Arrange Your Love Marriage

Arrange Your Love Marriage

A guide to understanding relationships and choosing your partner

Meera Ravi

Viva Books

New Delhi | Mumbai | Chennai | Kolkata | Bangalore | Hyderabad | Kochi | Guwahati

First Published 2010

Viva Books Private Limited

4737/23, Ansari Road, Daryaganj, New Delhi 110 002
Tel. 42242200, 23258325, 23283121, Email: vivadelhi@vivagroupindia.net

76, Service Industries, Shirvane, Sector 1, Nerul, Navi Mumbai 400 706
Tel. 27721273, 27721274, Email: vivamumbai@vivagroupindia.net

Jamals Fazal Chambers, 26 Greams Road, Chennai 600 006
Tel. 28294241, 28290304, Email: vivachennai@vivagroupindia.net

B-103, Jindal Towers, 21/1A/3 Darga Road, Kolkata 700 017
Tel. 22816713, Email: vivakolkata@vivagroupindia.net

7, GF, Sovereign Park Aptts., 56-58, K. R. Road, Basavanagudi, Bangalore 560 004
Tel. 26607409, Email: vivabangalore@vivagroupindia.net

101-102, Moghal Marc Apartments, 3-4-637 to 641, Narayanguda, Hyderabad 500 029
Tel. 27564481, Email: vivahyderabad@vivagroupindia.net

First Floor, Beevi Towers, SRM Road, Kaloor, Kochi 682 018
Tel. 0484-2403055, 2403056, Email: vivakochi@vivagroupindia.net

232, GNB Road, Beside UCO Bank, Silpukhuri, Guwahati 781 003
Tel. 0361-2666386, Email: vivaguwahati@vivagroupindia.net

www.vivagroupindia.com

ISBN: 978-81-309-1470-1

Published by Vinod Vasishtha for Viva Books Private Limited
4737/23 Ansari Road, Daryaganj, New Delhi 110 002

Printed & bound by Sanat Printers, Kundli 131028

Contents

Acknowledgements

I am grateful to all the people with whom I discussed this book for their inputs. I would like to make a special mention of Arundathi Harikrishna who validated the concept which encouraged me to write the book; Mamtha Rajesh who gave her valuable suggestions; Padma Dasari who supported me extensively by discussing various aspects and sharing her rich experience; and Sarita Bery who offered a much needed non-counsellor perspective. I thank all of them whole heartedly.

I am grateful to my family who silently tolerated my affair with my laptop during the period I was writing the book.

My special thanks to Mr Vinod Vasishtha of Viva Books whose unconditional support keeps me enthusiastic about writing.

Preface

Marriages may be made in heaven – but they need to be understood, nurtured and sustained on earth and in the absence of any of these, they are broken on earth itself.

Conflicts and disagreements are a part of any intimate relationship. But when the couple begins to perceive conflicts as unbearable and irresolvable, they may begin to wonder about the continuation of their relationship. Some couples are forced to live under the same roof due to certain obligations. Marriage per se may last but lasting does not mean loving. As a practising counsellor, I have come across quite a few couples who are in loveless marriages. Reasons may be many, but the end result is that they feel stuck. Some of them regret that they were not given the freedom to choose their partner whereas some others who had such an opportunity did not seem to have adequate knowledge on how to go about it. The end result is an unhappy life.

How did I conceive the idea of this book?

I know innumerable couples who spent ample time with each other during courtship but began facing problems pretty early in their married life. Some of the statements made by these couples go like this:

- 'What I thought was love doesn't seem like "love" any more.'
- 'I don't know what I saw that I fell for her.'
- 'Even in my wildest dreams I had never anticipated this kind of behaviour from her.'
- 'I don't think I know this person. I feel I married a stranger.'

With many couples (married and to be married) who came to me for counselling, I sensed that they struggled with the fundamental understanding of a relationship. During the counselling process, we would explore what happened, why it happened and how to mend the damage. At times I would give them homework (exercises linked to thinking and writing) and at the end of the therapy ask them to come out with an action plan for future.

Then the idea dawned on me to crystallize some of these thoughts and information into a concise, easy and systematic form which may be easily put into practice by a common man. This is how I started transferring my ideas onto my computer and as I reviewed it from time to time, I kept adding related topics. I would have liked it to be brief but everything is so interconnected that I just couldn't help but include all of them.

I have used some case studies while taking utmost care to protect the identity of the clients. Any similarity hence is simply coincidental.

What do I want to achieve by this book?

I have written this book for a number of reasons:

- To offer guidance to youngsters who are in the process of choosing their life partners.
- To help couples who are already in a relationship to assess their relationship.
- To help couples to improve their relationship.

And then there is also my heartfelt desire:

- To reiterate the message that the process of counselling can transform lives. If you have any queries regarding 'counselling' I suggest you read my earlier book, *Counselling: What, Why and How* which deals with each and every aspect of counselling.

As far as possible I have tried to maintain a very simple way of explaining my ideas throughout the book. If at all you find any technical term, it would be in the absence of a simple equivalent term.

As one goes about reading this book, it's possible that he/she may need to clarify his/her doubts. Seeking professional help is a wise idea. Some youngsters confessed that they hesitated talking to a professional counsellor for fear of exposing their relationship. It is far better to take the risk of opening oneself to a professional counsellor than jeopardizing one's happiness for life. A professional counsellor will maintain absolute confidentiality and facilitate a person not only to take the right decision but also for the right reason.

A Simple Exercise

As a prelude to reading the book I would like you to do a simple exercise.

On a blank sheet of paper, I would like you to define *'marriage'*.

You may begin with *'Marriage to me is...*

Let the thoughts just flow. Write whatever comes to your mind.

No time limit and no limit on the number of words.

Do not think logically about what you should or should not write.

There is no right or wrong way of looking at it; your thoughts just speak about your beliefs and perception of marriage. If you have close friends who would be willing to do the same exercise, compare notes to see how each ones' understanding of marriage is unique.

1. Marriage: An Introduction

'A successful marriage requires falling in love many times, always with the same person.'

Mignon McLaughlin

Marriage can be one of the most rewarding experiences in life. Sharing one's life with someone on an intimate level can bring true joy. On the other hand, a difficult marriage can cause heartache and pain. When two people get together there is a certain dynamic taking place. There are influences all around that can drag people down. In a relationship like marriage, there are internal and external forces that can either make or break it. Those who have discovered the joy of a successful marriage can attest to the peace and wholeness it brings to the couple. Unfortunately, there are numerous couples who do not ever experience that joy and wish that things could be different. In a majority of the instances we can see that as individuals they are all wonderful human beings, it is the relationship with each other that turns bad.

These days quite a few young adults are selecting life partners on their own. They most probably will choose someone from their school/college friends or office colleagues. Because they get more chances to interact with the opposite gender more often, it provides them an opportunity to get to know each other well. It is more than likely that they may start liking someone very dearly. The feelings may get stronger with the fact that they have subtle permission (or at least no strong opposition) from their parents. There are many things that go into taking a considered decision before proposing marriage to the person – this book will assist a person with gaining that knowledge.

The best way to educate oneself, of course, is premarital counselling but it is still in its infancy. I am hoping that this book would give much needed assistance to young adults to make the right choices and save themselves the heartache of making disastrous decisions in choosing their life partners.

2. Choosing the Special Person

> 'People shop for a bathing suit with more care than they do a husband or wife. The rules are the same. Look for something you'll feel comfortable wearing. Allow for room to grow.'
>
> Erma Bombeck

So let's begin! If one is given the choice of selecting his/her life partner, what criterion would he/she use? How will he/she go about choosing a life partner with whom he/she can continue to grow, laugh, have fun and share his/her interests and ideas year after year? If one chooses carefully and well, he/she will have a friend, a lover, a safe confidant and a soulmate.

Couples have a different outlook when it is an arranged marriage. Boys and girls know that they have to select one of the alliances that parents have suggested, so expectations are lower and adjustment and compromise come relatively easily. When they choose a life partner on their own, their desires and expectations are much higher.

Whether it is a love or an arranged marriage; neither of them comes with a guarantee tag. Both are based on empathy, responsibility, respect, commitment, love and trust. It is these qualities that make a relationship everlasting.

What would a person do if he/she is planning to select a car or a house? He/she would not go for it only by the physical appearance (no love at first sight); he/she would plan everything systematically to ensure it fulfills his needs. He/she knows what he/she wants, so he would consider all the features of the car/house, evaluate them from all perspectives to ensure it fulfils his requirement prior to the decision. After all he/she is making a huge investment so it better be the right choice.

Apply the same thought to the selection process when selecting a life partner because one is investing his entire life.

Despite making a wise choice there may be few problems be it the house or car, but that's more because of lack of maintenance than a wrong choice.

Though the basic principle of selecting a partner is similar to selecting a car or house, there is an intricacy involved here. In case of a house or a car he/she is going to get whatever he/her sees. There are no hidden agendas. Here comes the twist.

When choosing a spouse, the other human being doesn't come alone. With him/her comes baggage which consists of his/her personality, attitudes, behaviours, beliefs, values and characteristics. The baggage is locked and the person has lost the key. In fact that person himself/herself may be totally ignorant of some of the contents of this baggage because he/she packed it many years ago. These become the hidden aspects – surprises and shocks – for both the life partners.

A friend of mine used a metaphor to describe this. She said, 'Marriage is like a railway platform. Two people rushing from opposite directions, both carrying huge bags collide with each other blindly. Imagine what a blow it would be: both persons get hurt; bags get mixed up; everything (life?) gets scattered; and in a rush to move on, one of them picks up more bags than he had earlier. Only when he collapses due to the extreme load, he realizes that he was carrying someone else's burden too.' I find this portrayal very appropriate. In a relationship, it is essential for both people to be aware of their own baggage, apart from the fact that each partner should be observant to see the other's load, so both are saved from the hurt.

The guidelines given in this book would hopefully minimize such accidents and would help a person peep into those locked suitcases as well. This book may assist people with some basic parameters on how to assess who would be appropriate for them, what to look for in a partner, whom to avoid, how to identify certain problem areas and get what they want so at least they wouldn't be caught unaware. It would save them and their spouse from feeling sorry later.

Falling in love is a great feeling, but when you wake up with a ring on your finger, you don't want to find yourself in trouble because you didn't do your homework.

This book would help people do their homework well. The guidelines would help one make a careful choice. That does not guarantee that they will never have problems in their relationship. It goes without saying that once having made the choice one has to sustain the relationship. To do so, one has to nurture it, be it arranged marriage or love marriage. You have to keep servicing your marriage every few miles to keep it in good condition, thereby hoping to ensure a smoother ride.

3. Heritage of Arranged Marriages

'All weddings are similar, but every marriage is different.'

John Berger

Marriage is a socially recognized and approved union between individuals who commit to one another with the expectation of a stable and lasting intimate relationship. It begins with a ceremony known as a wedding, which formally unites the marriage partners.

Till very recently in India, elders arranged marriages for their grown up children when they felt that the time was ripe for them to get married. The parents weighed pros and cons of the various proposals they received for their children. The reasons for accepting a proposal differed from person to person, family to family and community to community. Even today some young adults prefer their elders to arrange their marriages.

The concept of love marriage was taboo as India had a tradition of arranged marriages. The idea which was once a taboo has become more acceptable in the Indian society. Children are now 'arranging' their own marriages.

Education and media has played a vital role in changing the mindset of people in India and now they have started thinking beyond the social customs and traditions of arranged marriages. More and more young adults are choosing their life partner without any kind of social pressure. In urban India, once a partner has been decided, it has now become common practice to permit interaction between the prospective bride and groom.

Most families now realize the importance of understanding 'would be' life partners and hence permit the couple to meet each other. The parents understand that there should be mental compatibility and understanding between the partners and this will happen when they spend time together.

My question is – when they are together – are they *spending time* or *investing time?*

Considering it is a golden period, which one should be utilizing proactively and productively, this book will help youngsters to know how they should invest their time and energy so they get acquainted with each other well.

I have become a huge advocate of a careful selection process when it comes to choosing a spouse. Couples can choose to lead a fulfilling life if they put conscious and constructive effort in this process. I remember one young girl told me, 'We have no option when it comes to our parents or siblings, we can choose none; But I would certainly like to choose my life partner on my own.'

4. A Marriage Is Not Built on Surprises

> 'The world has grown suspicious of anything that looks like a happily married life.'
>
> Oscar Wilde

Almost every marriage starts out as a huge celebration. Together with their family and friends, each couple is full of hopes and dreams for their future life together. But the road to a happy marriage is far from easy. Whether they are legally divorced or not, many couples opt not to complete the journey together.

Both of them need to know each other well, something that many couples don't actually do. In some cases, love's chemistry blinds people and by the time they open their eyes it is too late.

If they don't ask the right questions at the right time they may not only be in for surprises, they may actually be shocked. Sometimes it's not even *asking* – it's being perceptive and sharp enough to make sense of what is happening in their relationship.

I know three couples who split after marriage because in each marriage, one wanted children and other didn't. One of the spouses admitted regretfully, 'I never thought we were so much out of synch. I always thought he was fond of kids so I assumed we will have kids but he seemed to have no plans.' *They were dating for more than two years.*

Here's another example. After marriage this girl discovered that her husband's sister's family too lived in the same house. This came as a big shock to her. Even though her husband had spoken to her about them frequently before marriage, she thought they visited the family often. This was far from a pleasant experience. Even the house she presumed is his was actually in the name of sister's son, which shook the whole foundation of their marriage. *They were seeing each other for more than one year.*

A client of mine who was married for six months, *(after a courtship of three years)* said about his wife, 'She always evaded talking about her sister. I never met her before our wedding day. Few days ago I learnt she (the sister) is suffering from schizophrenia (a mental disorder that can be passed on genetically). I am shattered.' *These are all examples of incomplete homework.*

I recollect a client of mine (who came for counselling after six months of marriage) admitting, 'I think we wasted three precious years of our life while we were dating. We talked all irrelevant things. We never talked what we should have talked.'

It would be easy to blame the high rate of marital failure on things like not spending enough quality time together, nuclear families, changing lifestyles, failing to keep communication lines open. There's no end to books, articles and seminars that tell you how to improve these and many other aspects of your relationship. Despite all the knowledge, couples are not able to modify their behaviour simply because there are underlying causes. *To bring an everlasting change in behaviour, one has to address the underlying core issues which may be feeding the undesired behaviour.*

5. Story of Rahul and Anjali

'When negative feelings are suppressed positive feelings become suppressed as well, and love dies.'

John Gray

Rahul and Anjali came for counselling as they were having problems in their three year old marriage. Counselling was initiated by Anjali. I have selected some, out of the several complaints she had against Rahul, to narrate here.

The gist of some of Anjali's complaints are as follows:

- *He cares more for his mother than he cares for me.*
- *He does not need me. I have no importance in his life.*
- *He never shows any appreciation for all that I do.*

His response to the above concerns was:

- *She wants exclusive attention forever and in everything. Is it possible? Even if I spend one day in a month with my friends she makes a big issue about it.*
- *Her meaning of 'giving importance' is agreeing to everything that she says. If I disagree then she interprets it as not giving importance.*
- *There is no end to her wanting appreciation. It is like I have to make a time table and appreciate her or else she will get upset.*

Flashback of Anjali's life

When Anjali was three years old, her ailing grandmother came to stay with them. Her mother could not take care of Anjali as she had to attend to her grandmother. Before Anjali could even understand what was happening her brother was born and her mother got busy with the newborn. Her father was so busy balancing the finances, the kids, and his younger sister's marriage that he hardly could pay attention to Anjali.

Anjali felt neglected and began craving for love. Due to the illness, her grandmother became very short tempered and invariably Anjali was the victim.

Within two years of marriage, Anjali's aunt left her husband and came to their house to stay with them. The fights between her parents increased. At times Anjali had to be the little mother to her younger brother. She was always expected to be the 'good and understanding' child. Although she wanted to be like other children of her age she had no choice so she adapted herself to the circumstances and life went on. Fights between her parents stopped only after her father died when she was twenty.

In this whole story who is to be blamed?

We cannot blame anyone. They were all victims of circumstances. This background information was enough to know Anjali felt neglected and (probably) rejected by her parents. She had lost her childhood to circumstances. It was a matter of survival at that time and in the process her emotional needs could not be fulfilled. She felt neglected, rejected, fearful and angry. She grew up with low self esteem. If Anjali being a victim of circumstances was one bitter truth, the other was that Anjali's emotional needs were not met.

Anjali's internal process

At the age of three Anjali was not mature enough to think, 'Oh my poor mother! Look how much she has to work' or 'It's my grandmother's illness that has made her short tempered'. At the age of four she did not have the cognitive ability to process her brother's arrival among all her neglect. At the age of seven she could not understand why she had to share her chocolate and toys with an additional cousin who had suddenly appeared from somewhere. Anjali's little mind could not do all this processing.

Her childlike thinking was:

- *'Why can't I play with my mother?'*
- *'Why can't I sit in my mamma's lap?'*
- *'Why does my grandmother love only my cousin?'*
- *'Why can't my papa get more toys for me?'*

There was no one to explain the situation to her. She had to figure out on her own what was happening. Each and every time such thoughts occurred, they made her sad or angry but she had no one reaching out to her so she bottled up all her feelings.

Anjali's need for *acceptance, approval* and *attention* were not met because of the dysfunctional family. She was starving for twenty years and today she wanted everything for herself. She did not want to share that attention, love or importance with anyone. She did not know all this about herself till she came for counselling. It took more than three months of therapy for Anjali to realize her contribution to the whole situation. Here the underlying issues were Anjali's sense of rejection/neglect, her insecurity and low self-esteem.

Old Feelings Surface in Intimate Relationships

Experts opine, 'It's to be expected that being in an intimate relationship will certainly bring up fears and challenges from the past. These might include childhood fears of not being good enough, attractive enough, or even feelings of abandonment. If fears are not addressed they interfere in some way or another with the health of every relationship'.

People tend to make up stories in their head on the basis of some old beliefs. In Anjali's case her old self-defeating beliefs of, 'I am not important, no one loves me, no one cares for me,' .... made her create stories in her head which she interpreted as 'he does not care for me' etc.

We all like to think that we are in charge of our lives, but the truth is that a good deal of what we think, say and believe is part of the unconscious programming developed in childhood.

Whenever I challenged Anjali, 'Tell me what behaviour of Rahul makes you feel uncared for or unimportant?' She did not have a specific answer. She was creating those stories and there was no basis of truth to them. She could not change her thinking because she was overwhelmed by the old fears.

It's not easy to fight old fears and insecurities. It takes a process of first identifying one's childhood losses, accepting them, grieving over the losses (without blaming others), and coming to terms with the losses. Otherwise even if one thinks he has buried the issues and the negative feelings arising out of these issues, they are buried alive. Every time there is a trigger, the feelings inside get revived and the entire relationship starts wobbling.

Anjali was in therapy for ten months and by the end of therapy she could understand why she behaved that way. She then took responsibility for her feelings and behaviour, and worked on the relationship.

6. If a Child Lives with Criticism

If children live with criticism, they learn to condemn.

If children live with hostility, they learn to fight.

If children live with fear, they learn to be apprehensive.

If children live with pity, they learn to feel sorry for themselves.

If children live with ridicule, they learn to be shy.

If children live with jealousy, they learn what envy is.

If children live with shame, they learn to feel guilty.

If children live with tolerance, they learn to be patient.

If children live with encouragement, they learn to be confident.

If children live with praise, they learn to appreciate.

If children live with approval, they learn to like themselves.

If children live with acceptance, they learn to find love in the world.

If children live with recognition, they learn to have a goal.

If children live with sharing, they learn to be generous.

*If children live with honesty and fairness, they learn
what truth and justice are.*

*If children live with security, they learn to have faith
in themselves and in those around them.*

*If children live with friendliness, they learn that the world
is a nice place in which to live.*

If children live with serenity, they learn to have peace of mind.

Dorothy L. Nolte

7. *Influence of Family of Origin*

'We are made wise not by the recollection of our past, but by the responsibility for our future.'

George Bernard Shaw

This is a very famous and popular poem that reminds us of how influential our families can be. The way in which we are raised can truly determine the way we live our lives as adults. Each and everything that happened around us influenced us either positively or negatively. According to Virginia Satir, mother of 'family therapy', *95% of the families are dysfunctional.* The degree of dysfunction may differ but they surely impact the child forever. We do not exist in compartments. *Whatever we experience from the moment we are born remains with us in some form or other, be it feeling, behaviour, belief, value or personality trait.*

What are the characteristics of a dysfunctional family?

In dysfunctional families parents do not respect their children's personal freedom and privacy; they discount their children's feelings and may dishonour the child's boundaries. When parents disrespect a child's boundaries, the child's sense of self-his autonomy, self-respect, feelings of effectiveness and of making a difference are compromised. In place of a healthy sense of self, children may come to feel they are 'damaged goods': unworthy, inferior, inherently bad, incompetent, stupid or ugly. This negative conditioning limits what they believe they are capable of doing, being and having throughout their lives. It's possible that parents themselves may have come from dysfunctional families or they may be going through a trauma which creates an unsettling environment in the family.

Some of the reasons why a family turns out to be dysfunctional could be:

- financial crisis
- deprivation of any kind
- short/long term illness of any family member
- death of a significant member of the family
- parent/s unavailability to the child (either physically or emotionally)
- sexual abuse/incest
- parents experiencing any kind of trauma
- harsh punishment subjected to the child repeatedly
- not giving timely and appropriate attention to the child
- continuous fights/bickering between the parents (including cold war)

When one grows up in a dysfunctional family, the child experiences hurt from his/her parents' actions, words and attitudes (even though it is not intended to be so). This leads to some of the children growing up without a clue of how to relate to other people. These children may have the following hiccups when they are trying to establish intimate relationships:

- difficulty in accurately identifying and expressing feelings
- problems in forming and maintaining close, intimate relationships
- perfectionism, having unrealistic expectation of self and others, and being too hard on oneself
- feeling over responsible for others' feelings or behaviour
- having a constant need for approval or attention from others to feel good about themselves
- awkwardness in making decisions, feel terrified of making mistakes, and may defer decision-making to others
- exaggerated feelings of shame and worthlessness, and low self-esteem

- avoiding conflict at any price, and will often repress their own feelings and opinions to keep the peace
- acting violently to keep others at a distance

Having any of the above traits signifies that some/many of the emotional needs of the person are not met. It is advisable to first look within oneself to find the cause of trouble in a relationship before analysing the other person's life or behaviour.

8. Past and Present – An Overview

'We have not passed that subtle line between childhood and adulthood until... we have stopped saying "It got lost," and say "I lost it". '

Sidney J. Harris

Once a woman was preparing dinner, and her husband, watching, asked, 'Why do you cut the ends off the ham before you bake it?'

'My mother always did it this way.'

He knew better than to comment further, but one day he asked his mother-in-law. 'Why do you cut the ends off the ham before you bake it?'

'My mother always did it this way.'

Luckily, the grandmother was still living, so he had a chance to ask her, 'Why do you cut the ends off the ham before you bake it?'

'Well! Because my roasting pan is too small.'

Silly as it may sound, just as many family traditions pass on from generation to generation so are the actions and interactions between family members. Grandparents or parents may have had a good reason for their actions and reactions but the children, not knowing the reason, are imprinted with the behaviour, and dutifully follow through without examining whether it is helping them or harming them.

It can hurt a person to acknowledge that he/she comes from a dysfunctional family. It is comforting, of course, to think that the problem lies with someone else but it does not help. It requires a lot of courage to see the direct connection between our past and present. *Past is present.* It is always present with us. This is evident from the fact that despite best efforts people are not able to change their attitude or behaviour simply because they have not gone to the root of the behaviour and addressed the feelings that are feeding the behaviour.

We all have baggage that we bring into a marriage. In a sense, we all come from non-perfect families as none of us have perfect parents. When one wants to solve a relationship problem with a long-lasting solution, we have to bring the underlying issues to the forefront and confront them boldly.

Emotional Baggage

Emotional baggage occurs when we experience a hurt within a relationship and that hurt is not resolved or dealt with. We then internalize those negative feelings and develop fears that we may or may not be aware of. Over time, the same fears and negative emotions trigger negative or irrational thoughts and behaviours within us in another relationship, which then has a negative impact on that relationship. Taking stock of one's past can help a person in pin pointing where emotional baggage may be causing problems. Being able to identify the problem is the key to being able to put an end to it.

Blame is not the aim

We do not look at dysfunctional patterns in order to blame anyone, but to understand better our often inexplicable reactions and habits. Knowing where we learned certain behaviours, how they worked, and the beliefs we developed as children in the dysfunctional atmosphere can make it much easier to change and correct problem thinking and behaviour.

Deadly Ignorance

Before much was known about bacteria and viruses, many children died of diphtheria, a deadly disease frequently borne in contaminated water. Parents could easily have given their children the water that was fatal to them, without knowing. In this case, we needn't blame the parents, but the ignorance, for the damage to the children.

Family dysfunction is similar. Parents are often ignorant of the damage they're inflicting on their children through criticism, severe punishment, or neglect. In many of my clients' cases, the abusive and neglectful parents were treating their children better than they had been treated themselves. Moreover, if the parents knew any better way, they would have 'parented' that way.

9. Role of Unmet Emotional Needs

'No parent is bad; however the parent could be sad or angry and doesn't know how to be loving.'

What are emotional needs?

From the second we are born we have emotional needs. It is a deep desire within us which when satisfied, gives us a feeling of extreme happiness and contentment. If this desire is unsatisfied, it leaves us with a feeling of unhappiness and frustration. When a child is born he/she has some physical needs like air, water, food and sleep. In the same way he/she has some emotional needs which are as essential as physical needs. It is true that the child will not survive if the physical needs are not met, but it is also a fact that not getting the emotional needs met affects the child's psyche negatively.

Specific emotional needs

Following are some of the main innate emotional needs:

- to feel safe
- to feel loved
- to be cared for
- to be appreciated
- to be respected
- to belong
- to have a sense of autonomy and control
- to be understood
- to be listened
- to be touched

Who should be fulfilling the child's emotional needs?

Essentially it is the parents who should be fulfilling the child's needs but other members of the extended family/peer group or/and other adults around the child may also be contributing. In a healthy family the parents are able to get their own needs met in a healthy way and able to help and support one another in getting these needs met. More *dysfunctional* the family is, less the child will be able to get its needs met by the parents. In Anjali's case (The grandmother's long illness and subsequent ridicule by her, the mother's non availability and the father's poor financial status) led the family to be dysfunctional.

What will be the result of unmet emotional needs?

When some of these needs are not met for the person in the childhood, he may go through life feeling insecure, rejected, neglected or lonely. The child may grow up hungry and wanting, and his behaviour may be driven by this hunger.

Is there a way out?

Undoubtedly yes. If a person can recognize that the cause of the mess in his/her life today could be because he/she comes from a dysfunctional family he/she can go in for one-to-one counselling and resolve his/her issues. Counselling can transform one's life completely. It all depends on how much commitment one has towards himself/herself.

If you are troubled inside or if life just doesn't seem to be working, you don't have to just sit there and suffer. You do have a choice – you can choose to get help.

When couples come for counselling there are two areas that need to be addressed:

a) The problems that they have in their relationship with each other.
b) Their personal issues from their past – baggage which could be posing a threat to their relationship.

Without exploring both areas extensively it would be very hard to lay a proper foundation or resolve the problems of a couple in a relationship. To use a metaphor – if over a period of time a painful tumour has developed in any part of the body, the person may get short-term relief by popping a pain killer but to get cured completely he needs to go through a thorough investigation and treatment to get rid of the tumour. So even if it is a long agonizing procedure one may have to go through it in order to get permanent relief. Needless to say what the outcome will be *if the painful tumour is left untreated.*

Repeated Patterns Show Us Our Needs

For every habit we have, for every experience we go through over and over, for every pattern we repeat, there is a need within us for it. The need corresponds to some belief we have. If these were not a need, we wouldn't have it, do it, or be it. There is something within us that needs the fat, the poor relationships, the failures, the cigarettes, the anger, the poverty, the abuse or whatever there is that's a problem for us.

How many times have we said, 'I won't ever do that again!' then before the day is up we have the piece of cake, smoke the cigarettes, say hateful things to the ones we love, etc. and we compound the whole problem by angrily saying to ourselves, 'Oh, you do not have will power, no discipline. You're just weak.' This only adds to the load of guilt we already carry.

You Can Heal Your Life
by Louise L. Hay

10. How Do Healthy Families Work?

> 'Family faces are magic mirrors. Looking at people who belong to us, we see the past, present, and future.'
>
> Gail Lumet Buckley

- Healthy families are not perfect; there may be yelling, bickering, misunderstanding, tension, hurt and anger – but there is love and security too.
- In healthy families emotional expression is allowed and accepted.
- Family members can freely ask for and give attention.
- Healthy families allow for individuality; each member is encouraged to pursue his or her own interests, and boundaries between individuals are honoured.
- Children are consistently treated with respect, and do not fear emotional, verbal, physical or sexual abuse.
- Parents can be counted on to provide care for their children (even if they have conflicts among themselves).
- Children are given responsibilities appropriate to their age and are not expected to take on parental responsibilities.
- Finally, in healthy families everyone makes mistakes; mistakes are allowed. Perfection is unattainable, unrealistic and potentially dull and sterile.

I am neither implying that all children must have a perfect childhood nor am I generalizing to say all adults coming from dysfunctional families will have a distorted thinking. Not everyone who has faced pain and trauma is incapacitated. Strength can be forged in the fires of trauma and abuse. Some of the factors that determine the final outcome are the magnitude and duration of trauma that the family experienced, individual coping skills of the child and the support system available. All this would decide the extent to which the adult life of a person would be affected.

What I certainly mean is that when a person is not feeling powerful enough in his/her adult life to alter certain behaviour patterns/attitudes, (despite knowing that they are harming the relationship) it implies that something deep down is obstructing that change. Hence comes the need to look beyond what is visible – in the subconscious to see if there are unresolved issues.

11. Life Partner and Family of Origin – The Correlation

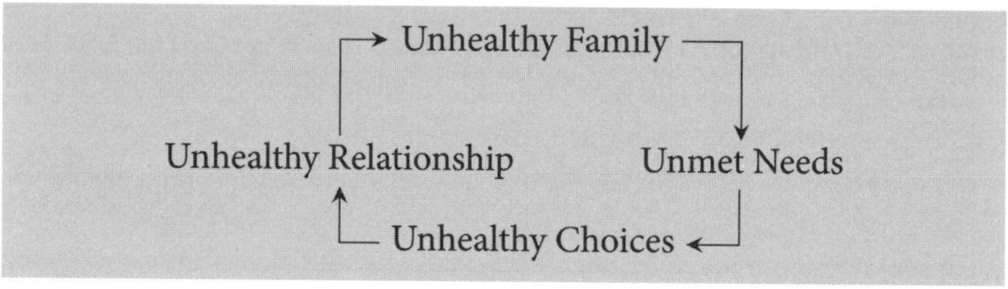

A dysfunctional family is not able to meet a child's emotional needs. As these children grow into adults, they are hungry and may have void in certain areas of emotional need. They may be unhappy, dissatisfied and disturbed adults. Their ability to recognize and take care of their needs has a direct connection to the kind of people they attract/get attracted to and the quality of their relationships.

The extent to which one recognizes and takes care of one's needs influences his/her ability to choose and attract well-suited partners. *At the same time, the haze of unmet and unrecognized needs can cloud one's judgement.* When a potential partner strongly meets one of his main needs, he may discount a lack of other important qualities, which will ultimately sabotage the relationship. This is one way people end up in relationships where there is more anger (hunger?) than love.

Once a person identifies his core issues, his thoughts and behaviour patterns, he can start the internal renovation – a process of mental house cleaning by throwing the rotten thoughts and beliefs, reconstructing new altered beliefs and re-organizing them to suit the present situation.

Once Mulla Nasaruddin was found by his friend searching for something under the street light. The friend asked him what he was searching for.

'The keys.'

The friend also searched for some time, and then asked, 'Where did you lose them?'

'In the park.'

'But why search here?'

Mulla said, 'Oh! It is bright here, that is why.'

Most of us, search for causes of and remedies to our problems elsewhere rather than at their root. Dr. Maria Montessori said, 'If you have a problem as an adult, turn to the child you once were, to find the cause.'

12. Who Are You?

'If you hate a person, you hate something in him that is part of yourself. What isn't part of ourselves doesn't disturb us.'

Hermann Hesse

The first lesson in choosing a life partner is self-awareness. Prior to getting married, individuals should know themselves. There is no such thing as *finding* the right person to marry; it is a matter of finding a person who is most appropriate to one's personality.

Self-awareness provides individuals with an understanding of expectations that they may place on themselves and others. Individuals need to be comfortable living in their own skin before they venture into marriage.

When we don't know who we are, we move through life on auto-pilot. We live by habit, reacting unconsciously to people and events around us. We generally let others tell us what to do.

When we discover who we really are, we take charge. We live with intention, focus and purpose. We wake up to the gifts in every moment. We uncover the wealth of creativity, talent and wisdom already inside us. As we become more aware, we see more clearly the choices before us, and claim our power to choose what's best. *We don't exist – we live.*

So how does one discover who he/she really is? Through awareness.

First, a person has to be clear about who he/she is; what are his/her values; what are his/her relationship requirements and needs;

and what his/her vision for his/her life so he/she can choose a partner accordingly.

Second, he/she has to choose a life partner who fits his/her vision and is compatible with his/her specific personality and needs. For example, say, a person realizes that he/she is not an assertive person by nature. He/she should think, what will be the outcome if his/her life partner, too, is not assertive or the other extreme, partner is very assertive and knows what he/she wants. What kind of dynamic would take place in that marriage? When choosing a life partner, one has to make sure he/she is able to resist the instant gratification impulse (sadly, highly encouraged in this generation) to react to the physical fascination natural in the beginning of any relationship.

As one grows in self-awareness one will understand better why he/she feels what he/she feels and why does he/she behaves as he/she behaves. That understanding then gives him/her the opportunity and freedom to change those things he/she would like to change about himself/herself and create the life he/she wants. Without knowing who he/she is, self-acceptance and change become impossible. *Self-awareness is empowering.*

13. Only a Person Who Risks Is Free

To laugh is to risk appearing the fool.

To weep is to risk appearing sentimental.

To reach for another is to risk involvement.

To expose your ideas, your dreams,
before a crowd is to risk their loss.

To love is to risk not being loved in return.

To live is to risk dying.

To believe is to risk despair.

To try is to risk failure.

But risks must be taken, because the
greatest hazard in life is to risk nothing.

The people who risk nothing, do nothing,
have nothing, are nothing.

They may avoid suffering and sorrow,
but they cannot learn, feel, change,
grow, love, live.
Chained by their attitudes they are slaves;
they have forfeited their freedom.

Only a person who risks is free.

Anonymous

14. *Parents Sketch their Children's Marriage*

'You are not responsible for the programming you picked up in childhood. However, as an adult, you are one hundred percent responsible for fixing it.'

Ken Keyes, Jr.

Whether one's parents had a blissful bond, or whether they struggled through their marriage. The way they expressed their love for one another – or didn't – throughout one's childhood, serves as the first model for what marriage looks like. And good or bad, their marriage leaves an indelible impression, leading one to decide what behaviours and gestures one wants to replicate in his/her own relationship.

When I asked a client of mine, 'How do you perceive your parents' marriage?' she said, 'My mom often grumbled that marriage had ruined her life. Every time she got upset she would say she preferred to die than to live in that hell.' Not only did my client confess that she got married to the first guy she met, to be away from that 'hell' but also accepted the fact that deep down her belief, 'marriage ruins life' could have contributed to her attitude towards her own marriage. (Needless to say this is an unconscious process)

There's no way around the influence our parents have on our life. The way they lived life, their marriage, style of parenting, attitude towards money and even style of communication influences what we do in our own life. Some of the things are good, some not. Either way, we can't completely escape their influence.

If one's parents were happily married, he saw how two different people can somehow manage to live a life together. But if one grew up wondering why his/her parents couldn't be happy together, that doesn't mean he is doomed to have a failed relationship. Many couples promise themselves that they'll avoid all the mistakes their parents made, which can lead to dogged commitment.

Nothing is etched in stone

The most interesting part about ones' parent's marriage is that the perception of one marriage is diverse among siblings and each sibling chooses to learn different things from each parent as well. Truly, there is no standard equation when it comes to human behaviour. Each one has to figure out the whys and hows of his/her life all by himself/herself since it is completely individualistic.

Yet again, counselling comes into the picture. When one realizes that a learnt belief, value or behaviour pattern is unhelpful in the married life, then with the help of counselling he/she can alter that and accomplish the desired relationship. So to conclude let me say parents draw only a sketch, which one can erase and modify to give it the preferred shape.

This is the story of two brothers. One was a drug addict and a drunkard who frequently beat up his family. The other one was a very successful businessman who was respected in society and had a wonderful family. Some people wanted to find out why two brothers from the same parents, brought up in the same environment, could be so different.

The first one was asked, 'How come you do what you do? You are a drug addict, a drunkard and you beat your family. What motivates you?' he said, 'My father'. They asked 'What about your father?' The reply was, 'My father was a drug addict, a drunkard and he beat his family. What do you expect me to be?'

They went to the brother who was doing everything right and asked him the same question. 'How come you are doing everything right?

What is your source of motivation?' And guess what he said? 'My father. When I was a little boy, I used to see my dad drunk and doing all the wrong things. I made up my mind that that is not what I wanted to be.' Both were deriving their strength and motivation from the same source, but one was doing it positively and the other negatively.

15. Enter the Dreamland

'Without leaps of imagination, or dreaming, we lose the excitement of possibilities. Dreaming, after all, is a form of planning.'

Gloria Steinem

Here's an interesting exercise.

Sit in an isolated and quiet place, without any distractions (doorbells, telephones, TV). Close your eyes and dream of your wedding day. Visualize each and every small detail. For example, what you would be wearing? What colour it would be? Where you will be? Who will be around you? How would you be feeling at that time? Let the feelings and experience just flow. Keep the eyes closed and visualize as long as you can.

Pen down your experience.

Next, visualize ten years after the wedding day. Where do you think you would be? Who all will be there as a part of your family? What will your home look like? What are the specific things you would have in your home? What would you be doing at that time of the day?

Pen down these thoughts.

The idea is to envision the scene and experience your feeling. You may have a mixture of feelings beginning from happiness, excitement and/or joy to fear, sadness and/or anxiety. If there are more negative feelings then one must try to figure out why is it so.

If the couple has been in relationship for long, they can do the exercise together. Each one can write the dream and then share the thoughts with the other. This would help the differences to come to the fore which would provide them a chance to discuss them further. In other words I am suggesting you to enter the dreamland together!

16. Why Do You Want to Marry?

> 'Take your life in your own hands, and what happens? A terrible thing: no one to blame.'
>
> Erica Jong

Too many people wed for the wrong reasons, which may explain why so many marriages fall apart despite the best efforts of those involved. There may be a lot of pressure and it can cause one to get into a relationship or marriage. It is important to realize that marriage is a lifelong commitment that lasts well beyond the wedding day. There are several things that one should think about, to make sure that he is marrying for the right reasons.

Some of wrong reasons for a person to get married and the subsequent thought process may be as follows:

- getting overage; 'If I delay more I may never get married.'
- biological clock ticking; 'When will I get married? When will I have kids?'
- peer pressure; 'All friends and cousins of my age have got married'.
- fear of losing physical beauty; 'No one will get attracted to me as I grow old.'
- parental/societal pressure; 'My parents are answerable to relatives/society'.
- fear of being alone; 'What if I never get married?'
- obligation; 'If I delay my marriage, my sister's marriage will get delayed.'

All the above pressures lead to desperation and any decision taken in desperation will not be a wise one. I admit, there are times when the pressure is inevitable but it is good to be aware of the reason for getting married and own up responsibility for one's choices. Owning up responsibility is helpful in two ways: a) the person may not blame others, b) that person may work towards change. *When you blame others, you give up your power to change.*

What is your reason to marry?

I want to get married because...

____

____

____

____

____

Having done this, one should ask oneself the following questions:

- Am I going through any kind of stress at this particular time? (If yes, you may not be in the right frame of mind to make good choices.)
- Am I a happy and contented person? (If not, you may be getting into a relationship with a lot of expectations.)
- Am I clear why I am getting into this relationship? Have I understood my own qualities and traits?
- How do I perceive my parents' marriage? (Unconsciously we all tend to pick up lot of stuff from our parent's marriage and based on that are our expectations on it. Its time to be clear about one's expectations from the marriage.)

17. Are You Ready for Marriage?

> 'It's surprising how many persons go through life without ever recognizing that their feelings toward other people are largely determined by their feelings toward themselves, and if you're not comfortable within yourself, you can't be comfortable with others.'
>
> Sidney J. Harris

There is a legend about a wise man who was sitting outside his village. A traveller came up and asked him, 'What kind of people live in this village because I am looking to move from my present one?' The wise man asked, 'What kind of people live where you want to move from?' The man said, 'They are mean, cruel and rude.' The wise man replied, 'The same kind of people live in this village.' After some time another traveller came by and asked the same question and the wise man asked him, 'What kind of people live where you want to move from?' And the traveller replied, 'The people are very kind, courteous and polite.' The wise man said, 'You will find the same kind of people here too.'

The moral is that we see the world not the way it is but the way we are.

Our 'self' or 'identity' is the private lens through which we view ourselves and our world. A foggy distorted lens means a foggy distorted world and a foggy distorted view of marriage. For some people, marriage preparation and enhancement can be largely meaningless until the fog and distortions of the self are identified and dealt with. In my opinion there are two major obstacles to a happy relationship, *low self-esteem* and *insecurity.*

What is self-esteem?

> Why compare yourself with others? No one in the entire world can do a better job of being you than you.

Self-esteem has become a buzzword. One can't touch it, but it affects how one feels. One can't see it, but it's there when one looks at oneself in the mirror. One can't hear it, but it's there every time one talks about himself. What is this important but mysterious thing? It's one's self esteem!

Self-esteem is the way a person feels about himself. Self-esteem affects one's entire life. *Self-esteem is an opinion not a fact.* These opinions are shaped by experiences in the family, at school, from friendships and in wider society.

Self-esteem is an important ingredient for a successful and happy life. Self-esteem involves our ability to think, to deal with life and to be happy. A person can be blessed with intelligence and talent but if he or she lacks self-esteem, this can be an obstacle in achieving success in a job, a relationship and in virtually every area of life.

Identifying low self-esteem

Low self-esteem can set in at an early age. Rejection at any age is likely to undermine self-esteem. For some this is temporary, while for others the effects are long-lasting. Some signs to determine if the person suffers from low self-esteem:

- **Lack of Satisfaction:** For people with low self esteem, the grass is always greener on the other side. These sorts of people are never satisfied with any aspect of their lives whether this aspect is their family or their car, these people constantly want more with the feeling that something bigger will give them the joy they desire.
- **Apprehension of the Unknown:** People who have low self-esteem are often afraid to try new things. Their fear of the

unknown prevents them from doing what they really want to do and achieving their full potential.

- **Staying in the Past:** Low self-esteem sufferers are constantly unable to focus on the 'here and now' they spend a huge amount of time bothering about the future and thinking about their past mistakes. These people often fail to enjoy the current joys that life provides them with.
- **Self Dissatisfaction:** Such people often fail to be comfortable with themselves; these people constantly focus on the negative and focus on losses instead of successes. They constantly neglect themselves or focus too much on their appearance because they lack the belief in their looks.
- **Acceptance of Imperfections:** These people are constantly unable to accept the fact that they're not perfect. They strive for perfection at all times and become increasingly distraught when they fail to achieve the superficial standards of perfection they set for themselves. These people are also over sensitive and worry about criticism at all times.
- **Lack of Intimacy:** These people can't be really intimate with other people and find it hard and impossible to be intimate with friends, family and other people.

Some more symptoms of low self-esteem:

- may frequently boast; exaggerate successes to cover up feelings of inadequacy
- eager to please; strong need for approval and constant support
- reluctant to express own ideas; lacks belief in self
- excessively anxious
- overly sensitive to criticism, but overly critical of others

We all indulge in above mentioned behaviour some time or other but if someone is crossing the healthy limit and it is impacting the relation then one must consider it as a problem area and focus on building his/her self-esteem.

18. *Insecurity – A Roadblock to a Healthy Relationship*

> 'There are many things that we would throw away if we were not afraid that others might pick them up.'
>
> Oscar Wilde

Insecurity is another big issue which gets in the way of a healthy relationship. It results from a sense of being unaccepted, disapproved, or rejected. Insecurity is the feeling of not being 'good enough', inadequate or incompetent. Everybody agrees that at core, human beings have an avid need for acceptance – for who we are – regardless of what we do and when that does not happen a person develops insecurity.

Insecurity is the foggy lens through which we doubt or fear that we will never be accepted for who we are. Insecurity makes us do odd things in order to make people accept us. People with insecurity would have a negative self image and keep belittling themselves with statements like, 'How can anybody love me?', 'What is the sense of trying, I'll never get it right!', 'Everybody is looking at me, just waiting for me to make a fool of myself!'. Insecure people become victims of fears that impair their freedom of action or choice. They have problem establishing healthy, long lasting relationships.

If one tries to find intimacy with another person before achieving a sense of identity on his own, he may be inviting turbulence in the relationship.

The good news is that both, insecurity and low self-esteem, once recognized, can be reversed with one-to-one counselling.

This would involve a process of identifying the events that could have contributed to it in the childhood, looking at it from an adult's perspective, and sorting them out – in a sense unlearning the beliefs that are unhelpful as an adult and re-learning new beliefs about oneself. It is a process of discovering one's true self.

19. What Are Your Relationship Values?

'A great marriage is not when the "perfect couple" comes together. It is when an imperfect couple learns to enjoy their differences.'
Dave Meurer

When one is interacting with people of the opposite gender and looking for someone special, the most appealing will be those who respond quickly. Some people may fall in love almost immediately. People tend to gravitate toward those with whom you have this 'chemistry' and who want to begin a relationship quickly.

Usually this process happens at an unconscious level. So by the time one realizes – chemistry has conquered wisdom. Love is more an emotional magic than intellectual commitment and we all know that magic is not reality.

There is a possibility of making mistakes when people want to move into the relationship quickly. People who end up in a relationship where there is immediate chemistry, where they are loved and adored immediately, should take a step back and spend some time evaluating the foundation of their relationship. It is better to take time to understand the immediate attraction and look for someone who has same values as you.

One should ask himself the following questions. I have given some optional values, tick the one which you find suitable. Each person may have his own values, apart from the ones given here, write them down.

- What do I need in a relationship; what can't I live without?
  Honesty/ respect/ care/ freedom and space/ trust

- What do I need from someone in day-to-day life in order to continue to love him or her?
  Appreciation/ validation of my feeling/ good listening/ understanding
- What do I value in someone above all else?
  Genuineness/ responsibility/ honesty/ compassion
- What will be important when I live with someone?
  Respect / freedom and space/ showing love and affection
- What can't I live with?
  Dishonesty / addiction/ instability/ financial insecurity/ insensitivity
- What is the worst thing a partner could do to me?
  Abuse me (emotionally, physically) / be dishonest / reject me / disrespect me

Once you come up with answers to questions above, you will have your own list of relationship values. Then, assess the people you are attracted to against your values.

Do not feel that one is judging a potential partner as good or bad. This is only to evaluate one's compatibility with people. What one may find unacceptable in someone, another may find lovely and extraordinary. Each individual must know what is important to him in a relationship. Then he has to find people who have the capacity and the inclination to provide it. After all, does one really want to spend the rest of his life living with someone who cannot give him what he needs? Real love, the type of love most people want in their lives, goes far deeper than attraction or chemistry. And it is worth the wait.

20. Chemistry vs Character

'Love at first sight is easy to understand; it's when two people have been looking at each other for a lifetime that it becomes a miracle.'

One married client of mine said, 'I think I married the wrong person.' Why this happens is because people tend to focus more on chemistry than on character. The theory here is, chemistry ignites the fire, but character/personality keeps it burning. *Falling in love is an event. Relationship is a process.* An important principle is, don't take a decision to get married instantly *only* because you're in love. Interestingly some couples who come for premarital counselling are stuck at 'we're in love'. They rarely have anything more concrete to offer. For many (if not all), when they say they're in love, what they may mean is they're infatuated. Infatuation is defined as a fleeting feeling for someone, whereas love is long lasting and is based on trust and commitment. Infatuation is instantaneous and some experts suggest it can be hormonal. *Love has patience* whereas *infatuation has a sense of urgency* and often that urgency fades. When marriages are based on infatuation; once the zing is gone, they assume they married the wrong person. One needs much more than the infatuation syndrome to make a decision to marry somebody. Some youngsters get so carried away by the chemistry of a relationship that they forget to really look at the personality and character of the person that they plan to marry.

I am not against the theory of chemistry but looking at other equations is equally important. Yes, sexual chemistry is an essential ingredient in a happy love relationship; but it is far from being enough to sustain a long-term relationship.

Romantic love puts us on drugs temporarily, suppresses our awareness of the negative traits of our partner (love really is blind) and creates a great expectation of the fulfilling of unmet needs and the healing of old wounds. We remain in this state until we are bonded and hopefully married or committed.

Then after the wedding (or just being together for a long time), the drugs wear off, the bandages are ripped from our eyes and we see our partners as they really are; critical, not available, unreliable, neglectful – remarkably similar to the negative traits we experienced in some of the significant people early in our life. This is where some conclude that they have made a major selection error. To get a clear and appropriate understanding, one should work on the relationship. Things can be set right.

21. The Story of Raj and Simran

Raj and Simran were married for one and a half years. They knew each other from the time they were in college. They fell in love when Raj was 23 and Simran was 20. They dated for three years before they tied the knot. There was lot of opposition from both sides (as they belonged to different castes and family statuses) but in the end they got married and went for their honeymoon. The problem began in this phase itself. Even after they came back they continued to have arguments which later turned into big fights. Let me give you a brief narrative.

Raj met Simran through a common friend and both felt attracted to each other instantaneously. They exchanged phone numbers, kept in touch and at some point began meeting. They would go for coffee, movies and plays. They would go for long rides on his bike and go for picnics with friends. They did have differences but they sorted them out. Life seemed like a never ending party. They discussed their wedding plans and they were on seventh heaven when their parents gave them permission to get married. Many friends were envious because they made a lovely pair.

During the honeymoon they had their first fight when Raj went off for boating alone because she did not show any interest in boating. Simran found it quite bizarre and they argued. According to her, he too should not have gone.

In her anger Simran refused to have dinner that night. Raj went ahead and had his dinner. Simran felt more upset. Next day they went shopping. She wanted to buy something which Raj found expensive and he objected. This triggered off her temper to such an extent that she started shouting in the shop itself. They had a big fight. The honeymoon got over.

Over time, Simran was offered a project which required her to go to another town. Apart from better monetary benefits, this was much better even for her career. She decided to take up the project but Raj was shocked at her decision and refused to move to a smaller town. He did not want to take a transfer and preferred to stay alone.

Simran went ahead. She visited home once in a month or so. Whenever she came she found Raj busy with his friends and he would hardly have any time for her. She started getting upset and during fights she would use foul language for them. She also began being nasty to his female friends. On the other hand Raj resented her doing well in her career. An added sour point was her spending money frivolously which Raj hated to the core and this lead them to split their finances.

Every time she came they had fights. Simran decided to quit her job without informing Raj. Raj was upset that she did not consult him before taking a decision. Their fights increased. They became hostile towards each other. One night they actually threw things at each other. That's when they decided to seek help. One question which they had in mind was 'What went wrong? We knew each other for so many years.'

This was only the gist of the story. I selected some incidents and shared them here without going into detailed descriptions. According to them the first six months of marriage revealed certain new aspects of one to the other which they had not anticipated.

The characteristics of Simran that were unknown to Raj:

- her temper and sharp tongue
- her possessiveness
- her independent nature

The characteristics of Raj that were unknown to Simran:

- his indifference to her career
- his being calculative in money matters
- his insensitivity to her feelings

Each one of them discovered new things about the other. They went around and had fun during their friendship of three years but did not make efforts to know each other at a deeper level. Everything went off smoothly during their friendship days as there was no reason for conflict. The truth is, you never know how strong your relationship is until it's tested. All too often, the stress of a crisis can pull a couple apartyſ]ou're sailing along through life smoothly, and suddenly you hit a huge bump. A serious illness. Financial crisis. A death in the family. Unemployment. An unexpected change. Then how both of you cope is the test of your relationship.

22. What Qualities Are You Looking for in Your Spouse?

Sometimes falling in love is the easy part, but keeping the relationship vibrant and exciting requires a unique skill set that, for most of us, must be learned.

What are the qualities you are looking for in a partner?

Caring	Affectionate	Sensitive
Tolerant	Helpful	Humorous
Honest	Expressive	Respectful
Reliable	Intelligent	Understanding
Adaptable	Straight forward	Organized

This is not in order of priority. If you would like to add something to the list, you may do so.

23. What Are Your Core Beliefs?

> 'It's not hard to make decisions when you know what your values are.'
>
> Roy Disney

Everyone has certain strong beliefs that aren't subject to compromise. These may involve religion, politics or personal needs. No matter how deeply you love someone these beliefs can't be given up. These then are your core issues.

For example children could be a core issue. One may want children, the other partner may not want children at all or one may love to travel all over the world but the other person may get sick at the thought of travelling. If one person is very religious and the other does not like visiting places of worship, it may cause trouble. I run through couples where one desires to settle abroad but the partner hates the idea. It would be a good idea to put down all your strong beliefs or wishes on paper. Some examples:

1. *I would hate my partner to drink.*
2. *I cannot stand a person who has a shabby appearance.*
3. *I hate people who are insensitive.*
4. *Integrity is a value I most want in a person.*
5.
6.
7.
8.
9.
10.

The key is to try and think a little more with your head and less with your heart. It pays to be as objective as possible when you are dating; to be sure to ask appropriate questions that will help you get to the key issues.

24. Relationship Appraisal

'The most important ingredient we put into any relationship is not what we say or what we do, but what we are.'

Stephen R. Covey

This is a test to know how both of you perceive each other. In this, one has to rate oneself as well as his partner. It should be done independently without consulting each other.

Is your partner ...

1. A good listener	( ) very	( ) not very	( ) don't know
2. Independent	( ) very	( ) not very	( ) don't know
3. Expressive	( ) very	( ) not very	( ) don't know
4. Sensitive to your needs	( ) very	( ) not very	( ) don't know
5. Levelheaded	( ) very	( ) not very	( ) don't know
6. Able to deal with stress	( ) very well	( ) not always	( ) don't know
7. Self-confident	( ) very	( ) not very	( ) don't know
8. Quick to get angry	( ) very	( ) not very	( ) don't know
9. Dependable	( ) very	( ) not always	( ) don't know
10. Honest	( ) very	( ) not very	( ) don't know
11. Fun loving	( ) very	( ) not very	( ) don't know
12. Caring	( ) very	( ) not very	( ) dont know

Once you have completed rating both for yourself as well as your partner, then compare notes and explore at three levels:

- Discuss where ever you see variation in your opinions. For example against the quality of *good listener* you have marked (very) for yourself and (not very) for your partner, whereas he/she has marked same way implying exactly the opposite meaning, then you need to find out why you perceive each other in that manner. Is there particular incidence which made you arrive at this opinion?

- Wherever you have ticked (I don't know), ask yourself – 'Do I really not know or I am afraid to express honestly?' If you really do not know then it's time you knew more about this person.
- Reflect on the kind of image you are projecting. If the other person perceives you in a totally conflicting way than what you think you are, it may be helpful to reflect, what is giving that image to people?

It would be interesting to discuss these ratings with a close friend (preferably who knows the other person) so as to get a different opinion. Another important fact to remember is that though basically we have certain qualities, we choose to use or not to use those qualities depending upon the person we are interacting with, the kind of relation we share with that person, our past experience, etc.

Behind the curtain

When one is gauging his potential life partner, it is based on what is obviously visible. There may be some aspects of his/her behaviour patterns that the person may be totally ignorant about. (Remember Raj and Simran?) So how does one know what kind of a person the other is behind the curtain? The answer lies in being perceptive and sensitive.

25. How Well Are You Investing Your Time?

Usually during courtship couples try to get to know each other and in the process tend to share lot of personal information and experiences. Here are some specific questions which would help you know your potential partner at a deeper level. While one is investing time in this relationship, talking about the following would reveal a lot about the other person. How intense the conversation turns out to be depends upon the willingness of both partners. Nevertheless, these discussions would surely open windows to some of the personality traits of the other.

Some of these questions to get to know someone may seem simple, but all of them will give you deep insight into the personality of the one you are asking. For example, in the first question, 'Where do you see yourself 5 years from now?', the answer will not only reveal the long term goals of this person, but it will also let you know more about who he/she is as a person. If he/she has big goals and dreams then he/she is the type of person who is proactive and likes to make things happen. If he/she has small plans or none at all, then he/she is a complacent person and most likely will be in the same position 5 years from now as he/she is at present.

And if he/she does not know what he/she wants to do then he/she is probably still trying to find herself/himself and figure out what life is all about. Such people may need more time before they will be ready to commit to anything.

Do you know?

- Where this person sees himself/herself 5 years from now?
- What is his/her most memorable incident from school life?

- Her/his goal in life.
- One thing that can trigger off his/her anger.
- What is his/her happiest memory?
- What is one thing that he/she would like to change about his/her life?
- What is the one thing this person wishes to change about herself/himself?
- Whom is he/she closest to, in the family?
- If he/she is in contact with his/her childhood friends?
- What is the one thing he/she likes most about himself/herself?
- What was he/she scared of in his/her childhood?
- What is the one thing he/she regrets the most in life?
- Name of a friend he/she hates.

I have not given this list of questions for the purpose of an interview. These are only indicative questions. The idea is that while spending time together, you may gently explore your partner through relevant questions.

26. Assessing Your Current Relationship

'To be happy with a man you must understand him a lot and love him a little. To be happy with a woman you must love her a lot and not try to understand her at all.'

Helen Rowland

This is for couples who have been dating for some time and know each other well. They have to answer in 'yes' or 'no' with a condition that if the answer is 'yes', one has to support it with an example.

Do you feel comfortable expressing your feelings and thoughts with this person? Even if you are repetitive / harsh in sharing your true feelings, does this person listen with patience?

Example: Yes because when I felt hurt by an action of my sister, I went to the extent of saying that I hated her, he allowed me to talk without passing judgment.

Is he/she a sensitive person? Does he understand other people and their problems?

....

....

Is he/she polite and respectful to people whom he/she does not have to be nice to, such as waiters, drivers, watchman etc.?

....

....

Does he/she treat his/her parents/other relatives with respect?

....

....

Is he/she a refined and cultured person? Even in the worst moods he/she will not use vulgar language.

....

....

Is he/she open to criticism? He/she is ready to listen calmly even if you give a negative feedback.

....

....

A few other points for introspection:

- Is there anything you are hoping to change about this person? *Does he/she work long hours or drink too much when he/she is with friends?*
- Is this person materialistic? *Is this his/her main aim in life? Will it affect your relationship?*
- What are his/her religious beliefs? *To ensure they don't clash with your beliefs.*
- Are your career goals similar? *What are your expectations from your partner regarding this?*
- Are you comfortable talking about financial matters? *Do you know each other's salary package/financial investments?*

Why I insisted on examples is because as humans our need for love is so strong that we sometimes allow our instincts and reason to be eclipsed by passion and hope. Although we know rationally how essential it is to get to know someone before opening our heart, many of us plunge ahead in our rush to have our dreams fulfilled. *Some questions given above can be discussed openly and the rest can be understood by observing the other person's behaviour (considering the fact that 93% of our communication is non-verbal).*

A Peek into Childhood

Since childhood is the foundation for a healthy or unhealthy adulthood, it is necessary to know few important aspects of the person's childhood. Casual discussions about memories of childhood, pleasant as well as unpleasant, can give you a peek into the other person's childhood.

Despite doing all this homework there might be areas which you would never get a chance to peep in, (e.g. his/her very personal habits). Yes it may be an acid test of your adaptability and tolerance, but the key point is no one is perfect and to expect a perfect partner is living in a fool's paradise.

I remember one woman client of mine had shared, 'He has stayed in hostel all through his life so he just does not know how to live in a home. He is repulsive at times and I cannot share the room with him'. To continue the marriage which was 'not so bad after all' they compromised to stay in different rooms.

27. Don't Marry Hoping Change

> 'Women marry men hoping they will change. Men marry women hoping they will not. So each is inevitably disappointed.'
>
> Albert Einstein

Some people marry expecting that the other person would change after marriage. I have often heard people point out that, indeed, people do change after they're married. Yes, they change but the question is – is it for better or for worse?

People have to be accepted for who they are. During dating, the most important question to ask oneself is – 'Can I live with this person the way he/she is?' Principle here is: *never marry hoping big changes.* If there's something that you don't like about the person, something that you may wish will be different in the future; you're setting yourself up for a potential mistake.

In the beginning of the book itself I said you have to ask the tough questions before you get married. Some of the things that people hope will change would be bad habits he/she has, like drinking, drugs or smoking. Don't expect the habits to change after marriage. Some people observe their 'would be' partner to be over involved with one's family and expect him/her to change after marriage. They should be prepared; it may or may not happen. If one can't live with that person the way he/she is, if one can't accept the other person the way he/she is, then it's worthwhile discussing those things and witness the outcome before marriage itself.

Some people expect; whereas some assume, that the personality traits or temperament of their partner would change after marriage. Some of the statements that I have heard are as follows;

'I expected him to mix more with my family members but even after marriage he did not and I felt really hurt' (A girl married for two years told me this.)

'I am sure when we get married, she will automatically start taking interest in cooking and other household chores.' (Assumed by a person who came for premarital counseling.)

'I will make sure he changes his lifestyle, even if I have to change myself in the process.' (Said by a girl who came for premarital counselling.)

'I never expected she will continue to be so short tempered even after marriage. I thought her temper tantrums would reduce once she is out of her dysfunctional family.' (Said by a man married for five years.)

You may call it a failure to realize that what you see is really what you get. I would like to call it *misplaced optimism*.

So are you geared up for it?

28. A Few Cases for Discussion

1. Medha, twenty-five, came for premarital counselling as she was unable to decide how to infer what was happening and was confused about her boy friend. The gist of what she shared was that he would often borrow things (mobile/vehicle/money) from his friends and then return them only after several reminders. A couple of times he borrowed money from her too. She used to find it pretty strange. One day he requested her to buy him an expensive mobile and that's when she came to me saying, 'Every time somehow he would convince me giving some explanation and I believed him. Today he is asking for a phone which will cost me a full month's salary, what will I tell my parents?' She was scared to upset him if she didn't buy him the cell.

What do you think Medha should do?

2. Albert, twenty-seven, came with a problem of not being able to understand his girlfriend. He said, 'I go out of my way to please her but she will still have something to complain about. She wanted me to stop smoking, I did. She disliked certain friends, I cut off from them. She wanted me to change my way of dressing (including doing away with my moustache), I agreed. I have been a slave to her but she still is unhappy. What should I do? I do not want to lose her. I love her a lot.'

What advice would you give Albert?

3. Nupur is twenty-one and her boy friend is twenty-nine. Both have been seeing each other for one year and are committed to each other. He is very protective about her and she enjoys all the pampering he does. They meet every week and spend hours together. Their relationship is going smoothly till the day he is asked to go to Singapore on an assignment. She is shattered. She is prepared to leave her studies half way through and go to Singapore with him because she cannot imagine life without him even if it is for a few months. She fears that she may lose him forever once he goes abroad. She is determined to go with him. He agrees to get married so they can both go to Singapore together.

Do you agree with their decision?

4. When Tanu, twenty-four, came to me she looked obviously disturbed. From whatever she shared I gathered that she was in a relationship for two years but due to some reason it did not work and they parted ways. It took her a few months to get over her break up, though she still spoke fondly of her ex-boyfriend. Now another boy had proposed to her and she was under confusion whether to go ahead or not. Although she herself confessed to me that this boy is very possessive, she wanted to tell him about her previous relationship. She wanted to be completely honest in her new relationship. Considering his possessiveness she was scared that in case he learns about it from some other source, he would be very angry or upset.

What should Tanu do?

5. Vishal, twenty-eight, was working in a five star hotel as a banquet manager and was earning a handsome salary. He had a girlfriend during college days but her parents did not

approve of their match so she got married to someone else. Then six months ago he met a girl and instantly fell for her as she looked a lot like his old girlfriend. She not only shared her name, she also had certain mannerisms which reminded him of her. He began meeting her on some pretext or other. They developed deep bonding and after six months he proposed to her. His parents were totally against this match as the girl was physically handicapped, but Vishal was adamant to marry her.

Should Vishal marry his dream girl?

29. Intermission

Dear reader
Let's take a short pause.

Are you still with me? Thank you for reading this far! Take a minute to think about some of the questions I have raised in the previous chapters of this book. Don't just go with the answers you think you know, spend some time actually thinking about it.

Being in a relationship can be a great experience but maintaining a relationship may not always be easy. The beginning of a relationship can be romantic and everything may seem perfect. Romantic love may be exciting and you may feel that you have found 'the right person'. Then after a period of time you may start questioning certain aspects of your relationship.

Despite doing the homework well and exploring all essential aspects of the partner, there may come a time when things don't seem to be working out the way you expected. What would you do?

Relationships change over time for many reasons: sometimes due to unforeseen circumstances; at other times it may be because the person's ideas have changed. It is possible that your needs have changed over time or the other person's expectations have changed with the change in circumstances.

Life is a process of change: One definition of life is constant change, but despite that we find it so threatening at times. Imposed or desired, planned or spontaneous, external or personal, change is: both an opportunity for growth and a source of potential stress and regret.

At first sight it might seem reasonable to diagnose imposed or unplanned change as the main cause of stress for individuals.

Paradoxically, it is often our failure to alter things to suit ourselves or to live with the new situations that upsets us.

Whatever the explanation may be and however well we may justify it, eventually one has to deal with it. The next few chapters would help you develop a deeper understanding of relationship and offer guidance on what course to take to lead a fulfilling life despite the 'change'.

30. Are You in a Healthy Relationship?

Sometimes it feels impossible to find someone who's right for you – and who thinks you're right for him or her! Then when it happens it is kind of unbelievable. You are in a trance. Everything seems just great. It's normal to look at the world through rose-coloured glasses in the early stages of a relationship. But for some people, those rose-coloured glasses turn into blinders that keep them from seeing that a relationship isn't as healthy as it should be.

Whenever there is a doubt of whether a relationship is healthy or not one must take a step back from the dizzying sensation of being swept off one's feet and think about whether the relationship has the following ingredients:

- mutual love and respect
- trust
- honesty
- support
- fairness/equality
- separate identities
- good communication

31. What Is an Unhealthy Relationship?

> 'If you made a list of reasons why any couple got married, and another list of the reasons for their divorce, you'd have a lot of overlapping.'
>
> Mignon McLaughlin

A relationship is unhealthy when it involves mean, disrespectful, controlling or abusive behaviour. Some people live in homes with parents who fight a lot or abuse each other – emotionally, verbally or physically. For people who have grown up around this kind of behaviour it can almost seem normal or acceptable. Let me tell you it's not! Many of us learn from watching and imitating the people close to us. So someone who has lived around violent or disrespectful behaviour may not have learned how to treat others with kindness and respect or how to expect the same treatment.

Warning signs

When either of the partners uses verbal insults, mean language, nasty putdowns, gets physical by hitting or slapping or forces someone into sexual activity, it's an important warning sign of verbal, emotional or physical abuse.

Have you experienced any of the following in your relationship? You …

- can't be honest about your feelings and can't talk about them freely with your partner.
- think you can make your partner's problems go away.
- are afraid of your partner's temper, so you avoid making him/her angry.

- usually feel unhappy and helpless in this relationship.

Your partner...

- wants to know what you have been up to in his/her absence.
- won't let you talk to others, even if they are your friends. He/she is very jealous.
- criticizes your friends or family and asks you to stop seeing them.
- decides how you spend your time together.
- has the power to make you feel terrible and uses it often.
- scares you by driving fast, drinking too much or doing other risky things.
- has threatened to hurt you or has hurt you even if he/she is sorry afterwards.
- makes threats about hurting your friends or someone else, or threatens to kill himself or herself if you don't obey or agree.
- pressures you to do sexual things you don't want to do and puts you down when you refuse.

Many people experience this kind of abuse in their relationships. If anyone has answered 'yes' to any of the above then he needs to evaluate his relation with this person thoroughly.

Some mistakenly believe that they can get what they want by controlling others, and that jealousy and control are signs of love. It is not so. Remember:

- You have the right to feel safe at all times in your relationships.
- You have the right to express your own ideas and say 'no' to something you don't like.
- You are not responsible for another person's actions/feelings even if they say you provoke them.
- You do not deserve to be abused in any way.

It can be tempting to make excuses or misinterpret violence possessiveness or anger as an expression of love *(the roots of such thinking goes to the dysfunctional family effect).* But it is not healthy. There are healthier ways of expressing love. No one deserves to be hit, shoved or forced into anything he or she doesn't want to do. When one is calm and at peace one should ask oneself – am I happy in this relationship or is it a burden/obligation?

I understand there is a possibility that some relationships may not clearly fall in either of the categories. I would say a good way to assess is to scale it on a scale of 1 to 10 (ten being the happiest).

Burden/ 1 2 3 4 5 6 7 8 9 10 Happiest
Unhappy

What is your relationship score? Is the happiness more than the burden? If not, then one must introspect deeper.

One young girl was controlled so much by her boyfriend that he would not let her talk to her male professor, he would choose which beauty parlour she should go to, he would not let her meet her male cousins or even attend their calls and if she did anything against his permission he would beat her black and blue. She swore by him and said, 'He does all this because he loves me a lot'.

An Exercise

There will be times when you would really like to end the relationship. But before taking such a drastic decision, do this exercise. Draw a line vertically in the middle of an A4 sheet. On the left hand side make a list of the perceived 'mistakes' of your partner; against each one write down how you responded or reacted to that. Once you are done with that cut the paper down the middle. Keep the list on the left side. Read the list on the right. If you see lot of sulking, screaming, withdrawing, it is time to reflect on your responses or reactions. it is advisable not to take any major decision until you understand why you behaved the way you did.

32. Regular Marriage Check-up?

'Love is an ideal thing, marriage a real thing.'

Goethe

You undergo an annual medical examination to make sure your physical health is in order, but what about your marital health?

Like a cavity that develops slowly over a long period, marital distress doesn't come out of nowhere.

Is it possible to have a regular check-up for one's marriage and assess the pulse of a couple's bond? A marriage check-up allows couples to catch marital cavities early on and take care of them. There can be two ways of doing it – either do it under the supervision of a relationship counsellor or conduct the marital check-up at home. Here are a few guidelines for a 'do-it-yourselves' kit.

Begin by asking yourselves these questions:

Are we honest about our feelings – and do we express it to each other? No matter how long you've been together, you don't ever totally know your partner. Check whether there are any hitches in this area and address them right away.

Are we constantly building a relationship reservoir? Every marriage has a relationship reservoir or the stored emotional energy of the relationship. Some of these are daily habits and are all very simple things. They help fill that reservoir. When there's a lot of positive energy there, you give each other a little pat on the shoulder or say, 'I'm so glad I'm sharing my life with you,' and you store it. Then, when the relationship is under stress, you'll have that reservoir of energy you need to get through the stressful period.

Are we harbouring negative feelings towards each other? There are times in a marital life when negative feelings tend to seep in despite best efforts. It is okay. The key is to be aware of it and work on it.

Are we happy and satisfied with each other as of today? The differences may come and go. Anger and irritation may be a part of marital life but at the end of the day if the couple were to look back and say, '.... nonetheless I am happy with this person', it would re-affirm that they are content with the core of the relationship. Then, if they explore at a deeper level as to what has been helpful and what has not, it may give them better direction towards their future together.

So what time period would you choose for the periodic check-up of your relationship – every six months or an annual check-up? Or perhaps a review just before you celebrate your anniversary each year?

33. Emotional Audit

> 'Everything that irritates us about others can lead us to an understanding of ourselves.'
>
> Carl Gustav Jung

'In any intimate relationship there are times when negativity seems to be overtaking positivity. At times people tend to magnify the negative experiences and /or negate the positive feelings. Then they are likely to say, 'He is always insensitive' or 'She is perpetually upset with me'. If a reality check is not done at this time then there is a chance that the person may start feeling overwhelmed by negative feelings. Here's an exercise for an emotional audit.

In the centre of a plain sheet of paper draw a line horizontally, every time there is an argument or a difference between you and your partner write your negative feelings at the bottom of the line. When you have shared good times or /and had a pleasant experience with your partner write the positive feelings above the line. Do it for a week to get a basic idea of where your relationship stands.

Put a tick (√) next to that feeling word, whenever the feeling surfaces. You may add words to the sample below.

Beginning Date........

Joy	(√√√)	Excited	(√√)
Happy	(√)	Satisfied	(√√)

Angry	(√√√)	Sad	(√)
Upset	(√)	Irritated	(√√)

Ending Date................

Once you are ready with your map explore it with the help of a counsellor. For example, a particular incident might have made you angry, but when you try to understand it at a deeper level, you may be able to understand better as to what caused that anger and whether there were other feelings (e.g. jealousy or hurt) underneath that anger. Further examination may help you discover yourself and your relationship more. Ask yourself 'Am I allowing myself to feel both positive and negative feelings towards myself and my partner?' Be honest with yourself while doing this exercise. It is very difficult to take an honest poll of yourself when you are in a situation where negativity seems much bigger than positivity; however I still would like you to give it a try.

A word of caution: This chart alone should not be taken as a final verdict on the performance of the relationship. It is only a guideline to help one explore one's relationship deeply. Unless and until one is absolutely clear about why he/she felt the way he/she did, no decision should be made. It is mandatory to examine and scrutinize all aspects of each feeling before arriving at a conclusion.

34. Ignoring Signs of Trouble

> 'More marriages might survive if the partners realized that sometimes the better comes after the worse.'
>
> Doug Larson

If your boyfriend or girlfriend gets angry with you easily and frequently loses control, it can be a telltale sign that problems in the marriage are right around the corner. But many people ignore the signs. Some youngsters see signs of troubled behaviour but think it will get better when they get married. Very often if this abusive behaviour occurs in the engagement/courtship period, it will only get worse after marriage, unless the person is in counselling or therapy. Some people think they will fix it after they get married. Anything that is mildly annoying will be extremely annoying after marriage. Interestingly, most of the times, it is an outsider, who can spot the signs of trouble in a relationship. Certain things are seen clearly from a distance. When there is a genuine suggestion from a well wisher don't discard it. It is worth taking a step back looking at it seriously to find out if there is any truth in that.

35. Relationship Destroyer

> 'All tragedies are finished by a death, all comedies by a marriage.'
>
> Lord Byron

Ever since the day we were born, we were forced to develop relationships with people. And we spend the rest of our lives bouncing in and out of different relationships but never learning how to make them work or how to improve them.

Almost everyone encounters some sort of relationship problem from time to time. The reason is simple: We are given absolutely no training!

In every other area of human development, we are given some formal training. In high school we were educated about everything: health, science, literature but no one ever explained relationships to us. We learnt it on our own without even knowing if what we learnt was right or wrong. So in essence, each one is left to fend for oneself.

Because no one ever taught us how to maintain a happy relationship, it's only natural to make some mistakes. Unless one knows how to quickly correct them, these mistakes often destroy the relationship. Ironically, these mistakes seem like the right thing to do. But if one is trying any of these common (but destructive) tactics, it is a process of slowly killing the relationship and pushing the partner further away:

- constantly reasoning out with the partner
- promising him or her that you will change (although you don't want to)

- quietly suffering hoping the relationship will survive
- telling him or her that love will take care of it
- begging him or her to change
- emotional blackmailing
- regularly seeking advice from friends and family (one would never know what reference they are speaking from, moreover the opinion may be biased for obvious reasons)

To elaborate on the last point that I have mentioned, let's create a story.

Aman and Naina, a couple, are having a huge conflict in their relationship. They have been married for four years and now are on the verge of a break-up.

Naina has two very supportive friends A and B, and a very close aunt C.

Naina shares her problems with A. A's advice to her is, 'Look no one is perfect. You have to compromise with everyone. There are so many people who have bigger problems. All marriages will have problems. You take care of yourself but stay in the marriage.'

Sometime later Naina asks B what should she do? B says with exasperation, 'Come on Naina! How can an educated girl like you stay in such a relationship? You are educated and independant. I think you should talk to his parents. Let them know what is happening or just pack your bags and leave. I am there, I will support you.'

One day Naina's aunt drops in at her place and seeing the worry on Naina's face, probes her about her marriage. Naina breaks down and tells her everything. The aunt gently consoles Naina and says, 'I feel really bad for you Naina. Anything you want from me please let me know. My only request is please don't tell your mom anything right now. She has struggled all through her life only for your sake. She will be so heartbroken if she learns that you are planning to break the relationship. Wait for some more time before doing anything.'

On the other hand, Aman, being an introvert does not like to talk to many people but he has a colleague (let's call him X) who has been a mentor and a confidant so he shares his woes with him. X has known Aman for more than eight years and treats him like a son. He was away on an assignment for six months and has returned recently. When he hears Aman's story he says, 'I suggest let it go on for some time. In the meantime opt for an outside assignment and be away which will give you time to think. She may realize your value then'.

Each person is giving suggestions from his/her frame of reference and belief. All of them mean well but it may not turn out to be favourable. It is likely that they both may get influenced by the suggestions or may feel more confused and overwhelmed. Ideally, before accepting any suggestion, Aman and Naina should clear the emotional fog that is clouding their thinking. This would enable them to see things clearly and decide appropriately. If they accept the suggestion without thinking about the consequences, it may be more harmful for their relationship.

Parents on both sides can be a blessing or a hindrance in a marriage. I have run into couples where either the extended family gets too involved in the marriage or where either the husband or wife struggles to cut ties with the parents. Parents ought to be involved in their child's marriage, as, often they have wisdom to offer. No doubt there is huge value in strong family bonding. However, boundaries need to be set, so that the couple can build the relationship on an intimate basis. If either the husband or the wife is struggling to maintain the balance between how much information to share and how much to keep under wrap, then steps need to be taken before small problems grow big. It is important to realize that in order to develop one's marriage, one must begin a new relationship with one's parents. 'Letting go' is hard for some parents and children as well and the ripple effect can be seen in their children's marriage.

Unquestionably there is immense value in the support from family and friends but if the problems persist, one should seek professional help.

36. A Conflict Is a Mirror

'All marriages are happy. It's living together afterwards that is difficult.'

Anonymous

Do you want to be right or do you want to be happy?

When people hear the word conflict, they often picture something very negative, such as fighting, arguing, bitterness and anger. However, current research suggests that conflict by nature isn't negative at all. It is fundamentally the experience of difference between married couples.

Just because couples experience conflict doesn't mean they don't love each other. Dealing with differences in opinions, goals, interests, desires, and so on, is a normal part of any marriage relationship. What matters is how couples handle these differences. Every conflict should be treated as a lesson. Once they have resolved the difference they should sit together and try to figure out what they learnt from the conflict. There is a learning entwined somewhere in there, be it about their need, their temperament, their hot button or their fears. If they can identify that, my belief is, it would provide them additional soil to nurture their relationship.

In a nutshell, a conflict is a mirror. Look into the mirror to see what is it showing about your relationship. Use the conflict to become aware of yourself and your relationship.

37. Listen to Your Frustration

> 'Consider how hard it is to change yourself and you'll understand what little chance you have in trying to change others.'

Frustration is a feeling of dissatisfaction, often accompanied by anxiety or depression, resulting from unfulfilled needs or unresolved problems.

Frustration, like any emotion we view as negative, has a positive side to it. We can look at frustration the same way we might look at a toothache. It's a sign that we need to take some sort of action. In this way, frustration is a tool for self-discovery and growth.

Frustration is a wake-up call. It is a different kind of frustration than what we experience when we are tired after a long day of work and the traffic is bad. It is the frustration that we experience chronically when we find ourselves in an on going bad situation like a stressful job or a bad relationship, and we need to make a change. Or, frustration can signal that we are due for a change in attitude and perspective about how we view our life. Let's look at both ways.

- **Circumstances/Environment:** An example would be feeling frustrated day after day with a job that is not challenging. Going to this job seems like drudgery and the days drag on forever. This is indeed a frustrating situation. And what is this frustration trying to tell you? It's telling you that you need to make a change.
- **Attitude:** An example of this type of frustration would be something like when you try to control another person's actions, or 'way of being', and the other person isn't complying.

This type of frustration requires a change in your attitude or perspective because what you are trying to do is simply impossible.

Being frustrated tells us that it's time to look at what we're doing and thinking and ask ourselves if this is working well for us. Fear of change or the consequences of taking action can sometimes keep us trapped in our frustrating situation. But again, like a toothache, if action isn't taken, we continue to suffer. This can lead to unhealthy stress in our minds and bodies.

So what can you do when you find yourself chronically frustrated? Ask yourself these questions:

- What is it that I find so frustrating about this situation/person?
- What outcome am I looking for?
- Am I expecting something to change outside of me, or do I need to look inside for guidance on what needs to change and how to change it?
- What can I learn from this (there's a lesson in there somewhere)?
- Is this something that is under my control, and if so, in what ways is it under my control?
- What steps must I take to initiate change and follow through?
- If my frustration is with a situation that is not under my control, what can I change about my perspective that will help?
- How would my life improve if I were free of this particular frustration?

I would caution each of us to remember that being able to blame another person for our frustration may answer some questions as to why this is happening, but we still have to look within ourself to find the right answers on how we should proceed. No one is going to do it for us. Sometimes it is very helpful to have a professional counsellor help you sort it all out to get past the bumpy part.

Sometimes you will have to push to change things. What do you wish to gain? What will it take? What are your resources? What are the consequences of not changing and what are the consequences of making a change? Sometimes changes must be made because the situation is simply unbearable. Change takes courage, even if it's for the better. If you're feeling frustration, you have been given a gift to look inside yourself and find a way to change your life productively, positively and in a healthy way.

38. A Date with Jealousy

'No one can make you jealous, angry, vengeful, or greedy unless you let him.'

Napoleon Hill

'It's not fair that Keshav always gets more increments than me, despite me putting in equal amount of efforts.'

'Poornima's children are so well behaved. I wish mine were obedient, so I'd look like a better parent.'

'How come even at this age Sujatha is forever trim and beautiful. I am doing all that she does but I cannot look like her.'

What is jealousy?

Jealousy is an emotion and typically refers to negative thoughts and feelings of insecurity, fear, and anxiety over an anticipated loss of something that the person values, such as a relationship, friendship or love. Jealousy often consists of a combination of emotions such as anger, sadness and disgust. Jealousy differs from envy in that jealousy is about something one has and is afraid of losing, while envy refers to something one does not have and either wants to acquire or to prevent another from acquiring.

Often, I come across individuals who talk about their jealousy with regard to various relationships, be it friends, colleagues, a sibling or other family members. Among clients many couples have spoken about jealousy with regard to their mother-in-law, sister-in-law, a close cousin or friend of the partner. This causes unrest in the couple's relationship. Jealousy comes when a person perceives either of the following:

- 'Someone else is getting more of ...(be it attention, affection, appreciation, freedom, success... the list is endless) than me.'
- 'Someone else is getting what I am entitled to get.'

Though the feeling of jealousy is the same, its impact is different. *Jealousy may cause a few scratches* in any other relationship (say between two friends or colleagues) but in an intimate relationship it *may cause deep wounds.* So in the following section I am focusing on aspects of jealousy that arise in a couple pertaining to each other only.

At times, the individual recognizes that his/her feelings are unreasonable with no valid evidence but feels incapable of getting over the jealousy. This is known as irrational jealousy as it is brought on by imagined or wrongly perceived events.

What causes jealousy?

Jealousy in and of itself is not technically considered a separate emotion but a combination of insecurity and fear. These make us act in defiance of all reason, sabotaging ourselves in the process. Jealousy is a manifestation of our fears and worries. Often we think that what causes jealousy is *triggered* by external factors. This is a common mistake. Whilst we are all of course affected one way or another by what we see and hear, the root cause of jealousy is always internal.

Jealousy is often triggered by low self-esteem or self image. The basic equation is that our entire world is filtered through our perception filters. If we have a bad self image, or don't feel highly about ourselves then our filters are corrupt. Things we see on the outside are changed and our emotional reactions are misplaced. I have already addressed this issue in the section 'Are you ready for marriage?'

What happens when we get jealous? Nothing endearing, nothing good.

'In a relationship, people think that by feeling jealous about someone, they are loving them. Jealousy is not love; it's the fear and anger of losing love. Intense jealousy does not prove there is intense 'true love' between two people. In fact, jealousy only reflects your intense needs, your desperation to keep what you want (at the moment), and your unrealistic (perhaps) demands about what the future should hold. Thus, jealousy reflects self-interest and self-love, rather than mutual 'true love.'

How does one know if he/she has a jealousy problem?

One might have a jealousy problem if either one of the partners does any of the following:

- Asking the partner a million questions about where he or she was, what he or she was doing and with whom he or she was.
- Not believing with the response he or she offers.
- Reading the partner's e-mail.
- Listening to the partner's phone conversations.
- Accusing the partner without any evidence.
- Getting violent or hurtful in retaliation of supposed infidelities.
- Threatening to hurt self, partner or others.
- Having different sets of rules for self and for the partner. For example, the boy can have many friends of opposite gender but the girl is not supposed to or if one partner insists on checking the itemized bill of mobile of the partner while keeps his bill under the wraps.

In simple words if one of the partners is trying to control the other or violating the other's boundary, or not respecting his partner's space then jealousy could be one of the possibilities. Jealousy does not have to cripple one's relationship. One can overcome the problem of jealousy by first acknowledging it and then working on it.

Steps Towards Overcoming Jealousy

1. Understand the emotions. At times it may be caused not only by the fear of losing something but also by anger that someone is trying to take away that you feel belongs only to you.
2. Allow yourself to actually 'feel' emotions in a healthy way. When you start feeling jealous, ask yourself: Is it more fear-based or more anger-based? Try going to the root cause of that fear or anger.
3. Communicate your feelings. Sharing your true feelings with someone without blaming them can create a deep sense of connection between the two of you and open up a dialogue about the path of your relationship. Use 'I' instead of 'you.' Instead of saying, 'You shouldn't have done that,' say, 'I felt terrible when that happened.'
4. Identify what your jealousy is teaching you. Jealousy can alert you to what you want and what is important to you. If you're jealous of someone talking to a friend of yours, personal relationships may be important to you. If you're jealous about money, you may have an underlying need for financial security. Ask yourself, 'Why am I jealous over this? What is making me jealous? What am I trying to keep? Why do I feel threatened?' When you begin to understand what makes you jealous, you can begin to take positive steps to maintain those things, without the cloud of negative emotion that accompanies jealousy.
5. Change any false beliefs that might cause jealousy. There are often false beliefs that underlie jealousy and fuel emotion. If you examine the belief, you can often eliminate the jealousy. Some common underlying beliefs are 'Everyone is out to cheat me' or 'If this person leaves me, I won't have any friends.' Beliefs are changeable. If you change your belief, you change the way you feel. Choose to tell yourself a belief

that is nurturing and supportive, and you'll feel better. When you begin taking steps to create a happy and fulfilling life for yourself, you will find the anger, the jealousy and the fear will disappear.

6. Learn to be happy with yourself and what you have. Stop comparing yourself to others. Everyone is different, and each person has good and bad qualities. Realize that you have the potential to create a better future.

Jealousy as a feeling is acceptable. It is a very natural feeling which we all feel at times but if and when the behaviour is driven by jealousy then one needs to take action. There's no reason to believe that jealousy will improve with time or marriage because jealousy goes right to the core of the self. Its roots are deep and it is not something that can be banished by wishful thinking. Sometimes jealousy can be baseless which can be termed as irrational jealousy. Irrational jealousy usually stems from one's own insecurities and low self-esteem. Address these issues first.

39. First Aid Kit for Your Relationship

'All married couples should learn the art of battle as they should learn the art of making love.'

Ann Landers

- a pack of patience – biggest pack available, *(to plug in and stop the flow of anger)*
- a notebook recording the qualities of your partner that you admire, *(which may be used to clean up the wound)*
- a directory of good times both of you have shared, *(which may be applied on the wound)*
- the kindest or most thoughtful gesture of your partner so far, *(use it as a bandage to cover the hurt, being visible it would act as a constant reminder)*
- a handbook on 'how to fight'

In a relationship one needs to keep a first aid kit handy as every now and then there are wounds, small or big ones, apart from the fact that at times some relationships need serious nursing care. In a majority of the couples, whenever there is an argument or disagreement, anger flows not only naturally but liberally too. Anger is a natural emotion. It is nature's way of telling us that something in our lives has gone haywire. Anger occurs as a defensive response to a perceived attack or threat to our well-being.

Whatever the reason, anger has to be expressed. Yet, aggressive displays of anger can result in violent eruptions that further hurt people. Suppressed anger, on the other hand, manifests in other ways and sabotages a relationship.

The problem with anger is that many of us have neither learnt to express nor learnt to manage anger effectively. Here are some rules for expression of anger:

Rules for expression of anger

Say what happened

Be very specific and say exactly what happened, when, where and how often.

Don't use vague terms or make guesses about the other person's intentions.

Say how you feel about it

Speak calmly, state feelings in a positive way and say how you feel about the situation and not the person.

Don't deny your feelings or attack the entire character of the person.

Say exactly what you want the other person to do

Request a small change, (one at a time), say what behaviours you want changed and most importantly ask for something the person can actually do.

Don't ask for too big a change or too many changes. Also don't assume that only the other person has to change.

Say why

Say how that change in behaviour will be good for you as a couple in a concrete way.

Don't threaten or bully.

Deeper Introspection

After both the partners are calm subsequent to an argument, it would help to introspect on the following points:

- Was there anything else affecting me before the argument started (for example, stress, anxiety, anger at someone else, hormones, tiredness or illness)?

- Were there any reasons I may have had for being defensive (guilt, avoiding saying sorry or forgiving)?
- Was there anything else affecting my partner (for example was he/she tired, stressed, feeling worried or upset)?
- What could I have said differently that would have helped to diffuse the row (for example, using less emotive language, changing tone of voice)?
- What could I have done differently that would have helped to diffuse the row (time it differently, listened more, not been so defensive, been more adult, not jumped to conclusions)?

How to fight?

One of the major tools in this kit is 'fighting fair'. How you fight is the key to whether or not you will have a successful, long term relationship. Fighting fairly in your marriage is a critical skill that you must learn.

Here's how:

1. Don't let little things that bother you build up until one of you explode leading to a big fight.
2. If you are angry about something and don't try to talk about it with your spouse within 48 hours, let it go.
3. Fighting fair means you know what the issue is. Then, both of you stick to the subject. Address only one issue at a time.
4. Keep your fight between the two of you. Don't bring in third parties like your mother-in-law, your partner's best friend or your sister.
5. Don't hit below the belt and don't bring up past history.
6. Respond instead of reacting and don't blame one another or make accusations.
7. Keep sarcasm out of the door.
8. Listen to one another fully while you fight. This includes watching body language. Look at one another while you speak.

9. Try to use 'I' sentences instead of 'you' sentences.
10. Be open to asking for forgiveness and being willing to forgive.

Be open to communication and remember that three most important aspects of communication are feelings, feelings and feelings.

Some Additional Tips

Don't Say Things in Anger: Don't say things in anger, because you'll certainly regret them later. Take a deep breath, calm down and, once you're calm and had time to think, tell your partner what's really making you angry.

Distance: Keep a certain distance between each other. Everyone needs some space and time to spend alone or with friends. Every now and then we need some distance from our partner, make sure that both of you enjoy the same amount of personal freedom.

Recall: Sit back and remember the time when you first met each other. Especially in hard times, try to sit back and recall the old time events and situations that reconnect you with each other.

Forgive And Forget: It is useless to constantly think about all the unpleasant events that happened during a dispute. Let them off your mind then and there. Do not be hesitant and be the first to forgive and forget! It can be a very relieving feeling.

As a conclusion, do not just simply sit there and feel sorry for yourself. Little things can build a better relationship and the big problems might not seem that big at all. To build better relationships you have to be aware of what needs to be done and especially how it is done.

40. Basic Principles for Good Relationships

Let's face it, if relationships are not d-i-f-f-i-c-u-l-t they are not easy either. They take time, effort and dedication and there is no guarantee things will work out in the long run. However, there are some basic principles, which help to keep relationships healthy and energized. Here are some of them.

Talk to your partner. Talking to your partner about all sorts of things, especially discussing how you feel about being together is essential. There is simply no way around it. If you don't talk about yourself, your dreams, your gripes, your fears and your hopes for your relationship, how would your partner know about any of these things? Your understanding of your partner and yourself in the relationship can only grow through communication.

Share power equally. The best relationships are those in which both partners feel powerful and heard. Remember that you are working together with your partner as a team. You are not running a race against each other. You only win when both of you are happy. If you manage to out-run your partner all the time, so that you win and he or she loses, you will both lose in the end. Relationships only work when both of you win. To make this happen, both you and your partner need to have an equal say in what happens. Dominating your partner or being dominated may feel safer in the short run, but will create a lot of problems in the future.

Be emotionally available. We all want to feel supported and cherished in our relationships. For that to happen we need to allow our partner to make an emotional impact on us. We need to be open to each other, rather than cut-off and be distant. For many people it is difficult to show their emotional side, their vulnerabilities as well as their joys. If it is so for you, you may want to work on becoming more open towards your partner. Being emotionally available means responding to your partner's emotional needs as well as being present physically.

Experience good times together. Relationships can get really serious and burdensome in difficult times. When work pressure builds up, children need things constantly and other duties are pressing, it is easy for a relationship to become a mere arrangement of convenience. In reality, relationships thrive on fun-filled moments spent together. Being able to laugh and joke together will build up emotional resources for the two of you for times when things get tough. Make sure you have some easy, relaxed and playful times with your partner. They will become memories you will both cherish for a long time.

Invest time in each other. Our lives are quite busy. Keeping up with work and all the necessary jobs takes up much of our time. Be sure to keep some time just for your relationship. You can use this time to reconnect with your partner and catch up with all the little things that are happening in his/her life. The time you spend together is precious, even if you end up arguing! At least the two of you are trying to get closer and work things out. Having time for your partner is essential!

Respect each other's differences. This is often a tricky one! When we fall in love with another person, we may feel that they are remarkably similar to ourselves. But as we get to know them and the hard work of the relationship really begins, we discover that they are totally different. We may try and change our partner to make them more like ourselves, but in the end we have to accept that they are different. Our partners will always be different from us. They think differently, and do things differently – and we need to accept this. Honouring that difference and even cherishing it will bring respect and love into your relationship.

Stay emotionally separate. Staying an emotionally separate individual is to keep healthy boundaries and not merge your personality with your partner's. Ultimately, we are all separate individuals and we all need to be able to manage our emotions on our own. Just because your partner is feeling something doesn't mean you have to feel it or automatically react to him or her. Staying emotionally separate is the opposite of a co-dependent relationship where both partners need each other to regulate their emotions or self-esteem in some way. This type of an enmeshed relationship is not healthy. Staying emotionally separate means that you take full responsibility of yourself and your emotions.

Show physical love and affection. We all have an inbuilt biological drive to touch. Additionally, we are designed to experience physical contact as highly pleasurable, reassuring and enjoyable. Spending time physically close together with or without sex is really important for bonding between partners. This could be any physical contact from holding hands, to hugging, to cuddling up somewhere together or to falling asleep in each others' arms. Make sure you do spend some time physically close to your partner. Both men and women need physical contact and sex is merely one form of it.

Don't avoid arguments. Arguments are necessary and can be extremely useful. There is no way you will always agree with your partner on each and every matter of real importance over the next fifty years! Arguing can be really productive as it means you both get to know each other and yourselves better. You may need to discuss an issue many times until all has been said, but as long as you learn something new about your partner and yourself each time, it is time spent well and will go a long way in creating a good relationship together.

Don't lose your individuality. Even though you're in a relationship, you're still an individual. You still need to take full responsibility of your life. It is your job (and not your partner's) to make your life satisfying, interesting and meaningful! It is OK for both of you to have separate interests, careers, hobbies and different set of friends. Relationships are about closeness with another, but that doesn't mean you can't be a person in your own right. When things get difficult in your relationship, you will need your own resources to support you through the tricky times. Having a life of your own outside your relationship will give you more stability and satisfaction in the long run.

Be honest and open. There is nothing as damaging to relationships as lies and withdrawal. If you find yourself hiding important issues from your partner or covering your tracks with stories, please reflect on what is going on. Your relationship will not flourish in the long-term if you are deceiving your partner. Be open and honest with him/her about yourself and your reactions. If you are struggling to show your real self, work at it! If you give nothing; and are not open about what you really think, feel or mean, then you are not giving your relationship a chance to grow.

Take responsibility for your own emotional baggage. Most of us work at this a lifetime. And we should. It is our responsibility to sort out whatever emotional baggage we have picked up in our past, including our childhood. Your partner may be able to help you with it, but ultimately we all need to sort it out ourselves. It is not our partner's responsibility to reassure us or make us feel in a particular way. It is our own responsibility. It takes real wisdom to acknowledge your own baggage and to resolve it, but it must be done! If you find it difficult, seek some help, but don't keep making excuses.

Show respect during arguments. Arguments can be extremely distressing and frustrating. We say all kinds of things to each other at these times and many of the things really need to be said. However, do not ever attack your partner personally! You may not like what he/she is doing, but that does not give you the right to call him/her names or put him or her down as a person. Fight fairly. Always respect your partner as a person, however angry you may feel about his/her actions. Attacking your partner personally will just make it much harder to resolve the issue you have been arguing about. Remember, only when you work as a team can you win and stay together.

It helps to apologize. Sometimes apologies are very necessary. An apology can put an end to ongoing disputes and ill feelings. I think that all of us will have, at one time or another, done something that we need to apologize for. Don't hold it back. Very often, your partner will really appreciate your willingness to reflect on what has happened and will forgive you readily. Apologizing needs to be supported by action to show that you really meant what you said.

Show your love. Last but not least, show your love! If you do not show it in words, emotions and actions, how would your partner know? Wouldn't it be really tragic to think that you care very deeply for your partner, but he or she couldn't feel it because you are not communicating it? It is good to show your partner how much you appreciate him or her. It will brighten up your days together and strengthen your relationship.

41. Is the Break-up Inevitable?

'Don't be reckless with other people's hearts, and don't put up with people that are reckless with yours.'

Kurt Vonnegut

When problems start cropping up in a relationship, a time comes when one draws a balance sheet to see if it is worth continuing. In case he concludes that it is not worth continuing it (at least not at the cost of one's mental health), it is time to make major decisions. At the same time, it is very important to avoid taking any impulsive decision. To ensure that the relationship has really got contaminated and can no more be restored here are a few questions for introspection:

- Do you really believe that a break-up is the best solution to your problems?
- Have you explored all areas before you have come to this conclusion?
- Have you considered the impact of the break-up on your social life/financial life/day-to-day life?
- Are you being honest with yourself?
- Are your expectations from this relationship realistic?
- Are you able to forget and forgive or do you carry grudges?
- Have you sought help from a qualified counsellor?

42. Picking Up the Pieces after a Break-up

> 'Relationships are like glass. Sometimes it's better to leave them broken than try to hurt yourself putting it back together.'
>
> Anonymous

Breaking up may be nobody's fault. It can be hard but sometimes it might be the best thing for two people to make the decision that they cannot grow anymore in this relationship. People may react differently when a relationship ends. It is not uncommon to feel sad, angry, disbelief, guilty and /or lonely. Managing these feelings may be hard. It may take some time to accept that the relationship has ended. Sometimes the ending of a relationship can give you time to learn more about yourself, spend time with your friends and do things that you enjoy doing. Having someone you can talk to may be helpful. You may also find it helpful to:

- *Keep busy.* Keeping active and doing things you enjoy may help to keep your mind off the break-up. You may want to hang out with friends, read a book, go for a run or walk or listen to music.
- *Try something new.* Sometimes it is helpful to make a fresh start by trying something different. There may be a course you have always wanted to do, for example drama, art, yoga or you may want to start playing sport.
- *Look after yourself.* It may be a difficult time and it is important that you look after yourself. Eating a healthy diet and doing something active may be helpful. It may also help to treat yourself. Do something that you enjoy.

- *Remind yourself that you are ok.* Think about your achievements, your friends, the people that have said good things about you and the things that you enjoy.
- *Talk to someone you trust.* Getting some support when a relationship is ending may help you work through how you are feeling. You may find it helpful to talk to your friends, your parents, counsellor or another person that you can trust.

Don't Pay Extra for the Emotional Baggage from a Previous Relationship

A lot of young people may have had a previous relationship. Though having had a relationship is neither uncommon nor something to be ashamed of, people sometimes bring some 'baggage' – emotional and/or health related – from the previous relationship.

Many people go from relationship to relationship without truly healing their hearts. They never discover what went wrong in their previous relationship and what they could have done differently. They keep repeating the same mistakes over and over again and expect a different outcome. Nobody does it consciously but it comes out like that.

Everyone must take time to heal their broken heart, spend some energy in taking responsibility for what happened, forgiving oneself and one's previous partner, and then decide what he wants from life.

If this is not done appropriately one may have to pay heavily for this excess baggage.

43. Relationship Autopsy

'To know when to go away and when to come closer is the key to any lasting relationship.'

Doménico Cieri Estrada

The outcome of a break-up may be different for different people:

- Some people may conclude that he/she is not fit to be in an intimate relationship.
- Some others may find the vacuum so unbearable that he/she may get into another relationship at the first opportunity.

Make a deal with yourself. Before you do either of the above, you must do a structured 'autopsy' on your previous relationship. This way one can avoid repeating the same mistake that might have contaminated the relationship and sealed the fate without even knowing.

By doing an autopsy, you take the mystery out of the train wreck. An autopsy can help one move forward with a healthy outlook and with an awareness of what can be different. Here's how.

- Identify what your problems and frustrations were in that relationship.
- Ask yourself what was your part if the relationship was not working (e.g. were you too passive, dominant, dependent, independent, aggressive, possessive, bad at communication, rigid)? Own up what you were responsible for.
- Ask yourself: What was my role in each of these? Own up what you are responsible for.

- What choices did you make that led to the results you got in your last relationship?
- You teach people how to treat you. Did you teach your partner to treat you badly?
- What do you want to leave behind from your last relationship? Only when you acknowledge it, can you take the steps to prevent repetition.
- You need emotional closure. It may be yelling and screaming, writing your thoughts down, or actually talking to your ex-boy/girlfriend. If you need to take steps to feel like you've stood up for yourself, do it.

Do not look at a relationship that hasn't so far worked out as a failure.

Often it's the seed of a current or past 'failure' that fuels one to the very success that one has always dreamed of. There's always something one can learn from every experience.

Past relationships give one a clearer picture of what one wants and what one doesn't want in a relationship if one takes the time to examine them.

Sakshi broke up with her partner after several years of turmoil. After the break-up, she realized what this relationship had taught her and that it wasn't a failure. This relationship had helped her to define the type of partner she really wanted to spend time with – someone who was not in a similar career, someone she could have a deep connection with and someone who was fun loving and outgoing.

If a relationship isn't working out, it is not a bad thing or a failure as the society usually labels it. It may be a lesson to learn and it may be time to move on to other 'lessons'.

This does not mean that one should take relationships lightly and throw them away at the first sign of conflict. What I am saying is quite the contrary. The purpose of all relationships is to help us to grow. Even the relationships that are the most troubling to us can be gifts in learning more about ourselves. Those people who really get under our skin can be our best teachers. It would help to look at all relationships as opportunities of growth and move forward consciously by learning from them.

Here are some questions to help you with this:

- What did I learn about myself by being in a relationship with this person?
- What beliefs did I let go of as a result of being in that particular relationship?
- How did it help me to move forward and heal, learn and grow?

44. *Common Myths about Marriage*

> 'For a married couple to expect perfection in each other is unrealistic.'
>
> Billy Graham

MYTH: *Romance will always be alive in a good marriage.*

REALITY: Nearly all relationships experience peaks and valleys. The everyday problems and challenges of married life can often cloud romantic feelings. This is when making the decision to love is important.

MYTH: *Marriage makes people happy.*

REALITY: You can't expect your spouse to be your one source of happiness. Your personal happiness must come from within yourself. Marriage can complement your own individual happiness but it can't be the primary source.

MYTH: *You won't have any problem if you truly love one another.*

REALITY: This is probably the most-believed myth about marriage. Love is not some magic which makes problems disappear. It takes nurturing, openness and commitment for the success of a relationship.

MYTH: *If you love me you will understand my needs without my saying anything.*

REALITY: Being in love doesn't mean one can read minds. People have to express what their needs are.

MYTH: *Conflict means a lack of love.*

REALITY: Conflict happens in every relationship. Fighting fair and not just to 'win' is the key.

45. Emotional Bullshit

Yes that's the title of a book that fascinated me and I picked it up instantly. As I started browsing through it I found it apt for couples. The author Carl Alasko talks about *emotional bullshit* as the plague which is destroying relationships. According to him, emotional bullshit is made up of three interlocking components – denial, delusion and blame which he calls the *toxic trio*. He has described beautifully how at times, in relationships people tend to unconsciously use this trio. He further explains:

- 'Denial – ignores or minimizes an essential fact – or a responsibility. Denial says – there is no problem. Everything is okay. You are exaggerating. That issue doesn't matter, it's irrelevant. (So I don't have to change anything.)'
- 'Delusion – creates an alternate (more favourable) reality. When things fall apart, Delusion says: Let me tell you what's really true. Don't believe what you see. Believe me. (This imaginary world I've created works for me.)'
- 'Blame – shifts the responsibility onto someone or something else. Blame says: You're the problem. I was forced to do it. I had no choice. Or, it just happened. Destiny willed it. (No one understands my true motives. Your accusations only make things worse.)'

In the example of the young girl (in chapter 28), she was in complete denial of her suffering; her delusion was that 'he does all this because he loves me' and she blamed herself at times saying, 'I should try harder.'

While talking about emotional bullshit on the dating scene he says that 'The following five basic requirements must be assessed without any influence from the toxic trio. No denial. No delusion. No blame. The five requirements are:

- *Physical availability*
- *No active addictions*
- *Financial viability*
- *Congruent values and ethics*
- *Emotional availability*

46. Case Studies – A Counsellor's Viewpoint

Dear reader

I am hoping you discussed the case studies I gave in a previous section. Following is how I would deal with each situation.

There is no prescriptive advice to these problem situations. There are many dimensions to each one hence not only me, no one can come out with straight cut answers by listening to the excerpts from a particular situation. In all these cases the person is seeking an answer which may be the basis of a major decision he/she would take. Considering this fact we cannot take the position of an umpire and decide who is in and who is out simply because there is a lot that goes on behind the scenes. So even before responding, one must see what is not visible and hear what is not being told. Besides when it comes to someone else's life we can only assist him to take decision by replaying the scenes and asking relevant question but his decision is like the third umpire's decision.

In the light of the above, these are some suggestions:

1. It is time Medha examined her relationship values to decide if she is okay with what is happening. Few questions for Medha to ask herself are, 'Am I okay with his habit of borrowing money/things?', 'What does it tell about my boyfriend?' 'If he continues to do so then how will it affect my life?' She must gather courage to speak to him. Fear, in a relationship, symbolizes imbalance of power. By keeping mum Medha is not only suffering silently she is also risking her happiness.
2. Although some adjustment is needed in any relationship, it does not mean losing one's identity. A healthy relationship

allows both partners to keep their individuality. Albert must consider if there is a possibility of his girlfriend trying to control him and if so why is he allowing her to do that. The definition of a healthy relationship is when both partners have nothing to complain about. He should ask himself, 'Am I happy doing all this?', 'If it continues where will I be?', 'Can I also make demands on her?', ' How long can I continue to do this?'

3. Nupur must have clarity in her mind about her life plan, 'What are my life goals?', 'Am I going to continue my studies or will this be the end of my academic career?', 'Either way is it okay for me?', 'What options will I have if I want to take up a career?' She must take the decision after considering all consequences. Both of them must look at the long term outcome of such a hasty decision. The desire to be with each other is natural but any kind of dependence is unhealthy. Nupur should also question her fear, 'Why am I scared that I will lose him?' In fact if they were to live away from each other for some time, it will be a good test of their commitment and stability and if there are fears about this, they both must address them.
4. If trust and honesty are pillars of an intimate relation, so are empathy and respect. Tanu must judge her boyfriend a little more before disclosing the information. Taking into account the fact that she perceives him to be possessive, she is taking a risk. Tanu should ask herself, 'What is the worst that's going to happen if I tell him or if he learns through someone else?' As I have mentioned repeatedly when there is fear in a relationship one really needs to introspect and evaluate the relationship. I would also encourage Tanu to do a relationship autopsy of her previous relationship to ensure she is making right decisions for right reasons this time.
5. It would help Vishal to become more aware of himself, his needs and his unresolved issues from his past relationship. It

is likely that he has not got over that relationship hence he is looking for someone like her. Once the emotional fog reduces, he may have better visibility of his future. Apparently this girl may be fulfilling some of his unmet needs which is making him cling on to this relationship. He should ask himself, 'How will it be to have her as my wife?', 'What possible difficulties I might have if I get married to her?', 'What is the foundation of this relationship – is it love or sympathy?', 'What will be my life ten years down the line?'

Asking someone to foresee what's going to happen or how one might feel in the future is not only difficult it could also be unsettling. People may not want to do so. On a freezing winter night, in a centrally heated room, snuggled under a cosy blanket, having a feeling of bliss, who would want to think of how it would feel to go out in the cold but the fact of life is that *reality bites*. He may have to; hence to be aware of it and be geared up for it, it is essential to think about all this. As well wishers and facilitators this is a gift we can give to our friends.

47. Relationship Counselling

Relationship counselling is usually considered as a last option for the couples on the edge of their marriage/relationship breaking up. Some individuals try counselling in the early stages when the first troubles arise. Counselling is undoubtedly something that a couple should not be frightened to try, even if the problems are comparatively small. Frequently, solving small problems before time with counselling can avoid bigger troubles in the future. Couples who got married years ago appear less likely to go for counselling, perhaps because it wasn't something normally practiced when they were younger and they may consider it as a disgrace but it is worth giving it a try. Younger couples are pretty open to the concept of 'seeking professional help'.

Ideally both partners should go for counselling together. It should be done in an accommodating manner. It should not be done to give the impression like one is blaming the other for needing counselling. Pointing fingers at the other does not help. Once they are in relationship counselling, they will be taught tips and methods for being better within the relation.

Whether you have been in the relationship for 3 months, 3 years or 30 years, it's never too late to try counselling to resolve problems. And it's never too late to try to stop small problems from becoming big ones. By facing any obstacles and solving these in the early stages, you're in fact making the relationship more secure in the long run.

However, if one partner is ready to seek help but the other is not, it is worth going to a counsellor alone and understand the situation from a different perspective.

48. What Is Premarital Counselling?

Premarital counselling is a good investment for couples who are serious about preparing for a lifelong marriage and not just a one-day wedding. It helps the younger generation to enter into matrimony with more awareness, clarity and understanding. It helps them to develop more mutually caring, respectful and lasting relationships. Everyone today has an individualistic approach. But, the key lies in adaptation and understanding. Looking at marriage realistically doesn't take away its beauty. In order to be loved or liked, all of us do things to make the other person happy. Problems arise when we are not primarily making ourselves happy.

Becoming aware, being mindful and being alert to issues allows early resolution. Premarital counselling helps young adults develop healthy attitudes and skills, to interact with their prospective partners respectfully and in appropriate ways, so that they can develop and maintain meaningful and fulfilling relationships. Premarital counselling helps people discover the real reasons why they want to be together.

49. A Special Word with the Reader

Happy marriages begin when we marry the one we love and it blossoms when we love the one we marry.

Dear reader

The reason why this book is in your hands is probably because you are experiencing that 'heady' feeling of love or you are experiencing the 'blues' of love; either you are contemplating marriage or it is some other reason related to your intimate relationship. Whatever may be the reason, I hope that you would have found answers in this book to some of the queries that are lingering in your mind at this important juncture of your life.

A man-woman relationship is a jigsaw puzzle. There are many scattered pieces that one needs to put together to get the complete picture. Having selected a life partner is one part accomplished. The book's main objective, though, is to offer guidelines to help you arrange your love marriage, there are many pieces that go beyond selection that need to be put together to solve the puzzle. That's why the second part of the book deals with understanding different aspects of a relationship. I added some topics which would be food for thought for all couples; be it married or to be married; whether it is couples who are on the verge of break-up or who are experiencing conflict in their relationship.

On the whole, human relationships are an intricate subject. It is not like the mathematical equation of 2+2 = 4. So while comprehending what is written in the book one must keep in mind that everything is tentative. There are no definitive answers. What solution works for one person, may fail, in a similar case, for the other. No two cases or situations can be identical. Each person and situation is highly individualistic.

This book is not meant to replace premarital counselling. My objective is to make people aware of how to select a partner, assess their relationship and lead a more fulfilling life. So in that respect, it may precisely generate a need for deeper introspection, for which counselling may be an option.

At *Prerana* we offer one-to-one sessions to further explore and implement the ideas and philosophies I have written about here, and to give you the tools to really integrate them into your everyday life. You may contact me if you wish to explore yourself and these ideas.

I am open to any comments/suggestions by the readers and there are any clarifications you can write to me without any hesitation on my e-mail: info@preranaacadmy.com.

Meera Ravi

References

You Can Heal Your Life – Louise L Hay
Emotional Bullshit – Carl Alasko
http://www.drphil.com/articles/article/316
http://www.suzannegold.com/
http://EzineArticles.com/?expert=Lee_Ann_Lambert
http://en.wikipedia.org/wiki/Jealousy

http://www.relationships-explained.com/pages/principles.html

Further Reading

Men are from Mars and Women are from Venus – John Gray
Five Languages of Love – Gary Chapman
Why Men Don't Cry and Women Can't Read Maps – Allan and Barbara Pease
Spouse – Shobha De
Forgiveness: How to Make Peace sith Your Past and Get on with Your Life – Dr Sidney B Simon and Suzzane Simon